Beethoven Unbound

The Story of the Eroica *Symphony*

Allan S. Haley

Eroica Press---Nevada City, CA
ISBN: 978-1-7327011-0-6
Library of Congress Control Number
Beethoven Unbound | Allan S. Haley.
Available formats: Paperback distribution

TABLE OF CONTENTS

FOREWORD

This book has been over fifty years in the making. Its first version dates from May 1966, when I submitted it as my honors thesis for a degree in music at Harvard. My thesis adviser was the eminent Beethoven scholar, Elliot Forbes, whose career work was a careful updating of the leading biography of Beethoven, begun by Alexander Wheelock Thayer and continued by Hermann Deiters and Hugo Riemann (*see* "TDR" and "Forbes" in References, pp. 140-141).

The purpose of my thesis was to bring to the English-speaking world of musicology the thorough study and careful analysis of a sketchbook Beethoven had used in 1802-03. Author of the study and analysis was the musicologist Nathan L. Fishman (1909-1986), who wrote in Russian. The sketchbook was in a State museum in Moscow, where it had been rediscovered after having gone missing during the first World War and the ensuing Russian revolution. As Professor Forbes told me, no western musicologist had any notion of what the sketchbook contained, because hardly any of them read or spoke Russian.

I learned to read Russian, made my own translation of Fishman's notes, had it checked by some native Russian students, and went to work. It turned out that the Wielhorsky sketchbook (after the name of the Russian count who had acquired it for his library after Beethoven's death) supplied the long-missing key to the genesis of Beethoven's Third Symphony, the *Eroica* (a name given by Beethoven on the title page of its first printed score – *see* Plate 1).

In the course of my work, I came to see that Fishman, for all his careful analysis and work transcribing the near-illegible sketches, had been either too cautious, or too politically constrained, to draw the principal connection which the sketches supplied between Beethoven's work on a series of four compositions which used the same musical theme. That theme first appeared in 1801 in the finale of a ballet score entitled *The Creatures of Prometheus* (op. 43), and for Beethoven it became the "Prometheus theme." He used it again for the seventh in a set of twelve contredanses (WoO 14) he assembled for Vienna's ball season in the winter of 1801-02, and then expanded on it greatly in a set of piano variations (op. 35) he completed in the fall of 1802, after he had spent the summer outside of Vienna in the nearby village of Heiligenstadt. Beethoven had specifically asked his publisher to call them the "*Prometheus* Variations" on the title page. That was meant as a link to Beethoven's Third Symphony (op. 55), on which he began work at

Heiligenstadt also in the fall of 1802, and in which he used the Prometheus theme for the finale, a set of boundlessly creative orchestral variations.

The thesis I developed in 1966 was that the figure of the mythological Titan Prometheus, who brought to mankind divine fire stolen from Vulcan's forge on Mt. Olympus, and whom Zeus then severely punished for his deed, had become central to Beethoven during the years 1801-1804. That was when Beethoven reluctantly came to the conclusion that he was gradually losing his hearing, and that the process was irreversible.

There was scarcely a worse punishment for a composer than to go deaf. Beethoven came to view his fate most bitterly, given all the wonderful music he had already presented to mankind, and which he expected to continue giving. It was an unjust fate, exactly as the punishment the gods meted out to Prometheus had been unjust. But in the ballet for which Beethoven wrote the music, Prometheus had come through his ordeal triumphantly (in the music we are calling the Prometheus theme). Beethoven fastened on that theme, accordingly, as the vehicle by which he would emerge just as triumphantly from the ordeal of his deafness.

I had expected that with time, other musicologists would develop the same thesis using Fishman's edition of the sketchbook. I expected also that the sketchbook and Fishman's notes might eventually be published in an English-language edition. But after fifty years, during which I pursued a career in law and winemaking, not musicology, neither has happened.

In my fortieth year after graduation, I decided that if anything were ever to be published on the Prometheus connection, I would have to do it. I took a leave from my law career to travel to Europe, to visit the libraries in Bonn, Krakow, Vienna, Berlin and Paris, to bring my research up to date. In the course of that work, my thesis expanded considerably as I gathered more background information about the ballet, its author and principal dancers, and Beethoven's time in Heiligenstadt and immediately afterwards.

This, briefly, is the story of the book you hold in your hands. It is composed at three different levels, intended to accommodate different degrees of interest. The text itself tells the basic story of how the *Eroica* came into being; the reader who wants to follow that story need never look at a musical figure, or endnote. At the second level are the musical examples. These enable the ones who read music to follow the details of that story as it evolved from the many sketches into Beethoven's finished works – a musicological thread that reveals the tremendous work that Beethoven put into almost every bar. And finally, for scholars and those with a deep interest, the endnotes and appendices have been compiled with an eye to providing all the background and commentary one could desire. (At the same time, the reader should bear in mind that this is not a biography of the composer, but a monograph on the genesis of the *Eroica*.)

I have many more people to thank for their generous assistance over the course of fifty years than I can now remember. I acknowledge above all my debt to Elliot Forbes, a lifelong mentor and benefactor; to James Haar and others on the Harvard music faculty who read my thesis and offered valuable feedback; to Hans-Heinz Eggebrecht at Freiburg who welcomed me into his Beethoven-Seminar; and to Paul Henry Lang, who gave me advice about publishing my thesis. I thank all the wonderful librarians who have given me untold hours of help locating obscure articles, illustrations and manuscripts – especially those at the Beethoven-Haus in Bonn, at the Nationalbibliothek in Vienna and its counterparts in Berlin and Paris, at the Jagiellonian University in Krakow (where the successor to the Wielhorsky sketchbook, called the *Eroica* sketchbook, reposes), and at the Eda Kuhn Loeb Music Library at Harvard. Finally, I thank all the wonderful friends I have made in music over the years, who have provided support, feedback and assistance, especially F. John Adams, Frfr. Isolde von Geyer, Pawel Skrzypek, Heinz and Ingrid Hochhäusl, Sarah Polzer-Storek, Alain Liègeois, and my Webmaster extraordinaire and man in Vienna, Rick Fanning, who has done so much to bring this manuscript to fruition. For the shaping of it into a published book, I am grateful beyond measure for the skilled and efficient help of the staff at NewBookAuthors.com, especially Em Hughes. Last but by no means least, I thank my wonderful family – brothers David and Brian, sister Janet, spouse Bobbie, daughters Sook, Sophie and Myfanwy, and son Andrew – for enabling me to spend so much time on this project without once complaining of neglect. May you each find in this book some small reward for having helped bring it into being.

Nevada City, California
August 1, 2018

Allan Haley

To suffer woes which Hope thinks infinite;
To forgive wrongs darker than death or night;
    To defy Power, which seems omnipotent;
To love, and bear; to hope till Hope creates
From its own wreck the thing it contemplates . . .

—Shelley, *Prometheus Unbound* (1820), act iv, 570-74

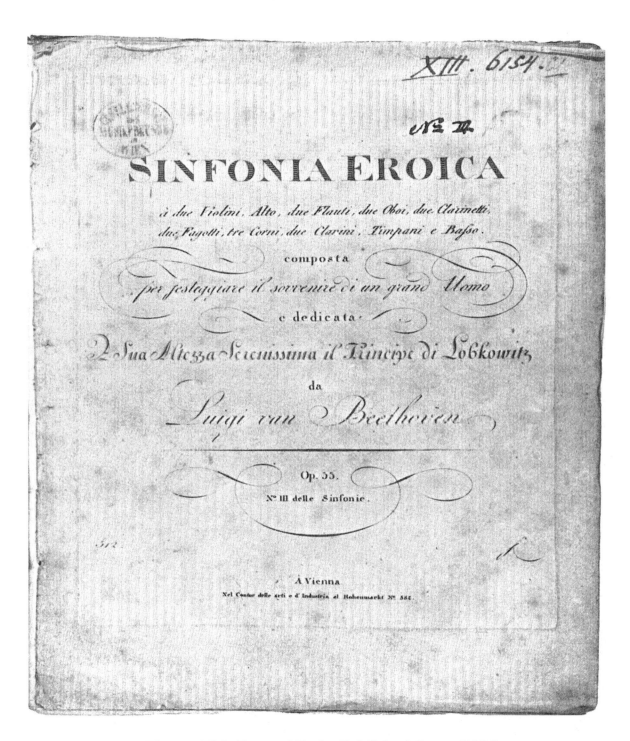

Plate 1. Title Page of *Eroica* Published Score (1806)

Chapter One:
Introduction

Beethoven's Third Symphony is one of only two symphonies that he entitled himself.[1] When the orchestra parts for his Third Symphony were published for the first time in 1806 (*see* Plate 1, p. ix), Beethoven called the work "*Sinfonia eroica*" on the title page and added the subtitle "*composta per festeggiare il sovvenire di un grand Uomo*" ("heroic Symphony / composed to celebrate the memory of a great Man"). The title page also carried a dedication of the work to one of Beethoven's most important patrons, Prince Lobkowitz.

The work has been called the *Eroica* Symphony ever since. But what did Beethoven mean? Who was this "great Man" whose memory he wanted to celebrate? And what is heroic about the music of the symphony? (Why, for example, is its second movement a funeral march?) Behind the answers to these questions lies a story that has never been fully told.

Part of the reason the story remains unknown is that a key source to its unfolding is largely inaccessible. In the archives of the Glinka Library in Moscow reposes a sketchbook that Beethoven used in the years 1802-1803. Beethoven kept his sketchbooks with him all his life,[2] and used them to lay out preliminary ideas for his compositions, which he then worked and reworked in further sketches until he felt ready to begin the preparation of a final score, or autograph, which would be given to the publisher for engraving and printing, or sometimes to a trusted copyist for further deciphering.[3] The sketchbooks survived the more than 50 moves that Beethoven made during his lifetime in Vienna,[4] and were included among the personal items auctioned after his death.[5] Although they were largely indecipherable, many buyers and collectors considered them valuable as having been written by Beethoven himself. As a result of the sale, the collective treasure which the sketchbooks represented was broken up, disassembled, and scattered first to the far corners of Europe, and from there to all parts of the world.

The sketchbook now in Moscow, called by some musicologists the "Wielhorsky" sketchbook after the Russian count who was first revealed as its owner some 33 years after Beethoven died,[6] was published in a three-volume edition in 1962. (*See* Appendix A, pp. 73ff.) One volume was a photographic facsimile; the second was a transcription of each page into conventional notation, and the third was a volume of analysis and commentary written by the book's editor, the Russian musicologist Nathan Fishman. However, because the edition appeared only in the Soviet Union, and the notes and commentary were entirely in Russian, its contents have received minimal notice in the English-speaking world.[7]

The Wielhorsky sketchbook contains drafts for compositions that Beethoven was working on in 1802 and 1803—chief among them the piano variations opus 35, which some also call *"Eroica"* because of their musical similarity to the Symphony's fourth movement;[8] the oratorio *Christus am Oelberge* (*"Christ on the Mount of Olives"*), opus 85; and various lesser works. However, immediately after the sketches for the piano variations, which he offered to a publisher on October 18, 1802, Beethoven laid out a preliminary plan for three movements of an orchestral work.[9] The first movement begins with a stately introduction in the key of E-flat major, which is the key of the *Eroica* Symphony, and transitions to a theme in ¾ time. The second movement is designated in the sketch as an *"adagio C dur"*, or adagio in C major; there are indications for passages in C minor as well. Beethoven titles the third movement in his sketch *"Menuetto serioso"*, or a minuet to be performed in a solemn, serious manner; then he returns to sketches for the first movement in E-flat. There are no sketches or plans for a fourth movement. The draft breaks off after filling two pages, and there are no other related sketches in the remaining 129 pages of the sketchbook.

If these sketches by Beethoven represent a preliminary draft of a symphony, it is striking how they parallel the first three movements of the *Eroica* in character, key and sequence. Beginning with the nineteenth century, and continuing to the present day, those scholars who have examined the sketchbook have pronounced them the precursors of that groundbreaking work.[10] It was only with Fishman's publication of the full book in facsimile and transcription, however, that specialists in the study of Beethoven's sketches could see the close relationship between the sketches on pages 44 and 45 and Beethoven's work on the variations for piano that fill the immediately preceding pages. Scholars are now mostly agreed that the reason that there are no separate sketches for a fourth movement is that Beethoven had already formed the intention to use the music of those variations as the basis for the finale of the symphony.[11]

In other words, the sequence of the drafts in the Wielhorsky sketchbook provides evidence (1) that Beethoven's idea for his Third Symphony came to him in the course of his sketching out the variations for piano, opus 35; (2) that he decided to use the work he had done on the piano variations as the basis for the last movement of that Symphony; and (3) that immediately after finishing his work on the variations, he laid out a plan for the *Eroica*'s first three movements, *i.e.*, he conceived the work as an entirety. His ideas for the Symphony, therefore, grew out of its last movement, which in turn grew out of his work on opus 35.

This is not the end of the analysis, however. After Beethoven had sent the piano variations off to be printed, he wrote the publisher and instructed him to ensure that the title page of the composition named the source of the theme on which he had composed them: a ballet he had written in 1801, called *Gli uomini di Prometeo* ("*The Men of Prometheus*").[12] Shall we then say that the genesis of the *Eroica* symphony lies in the ballet music for *Prometheus*?

It turns out that scholars are sharply divided on this point.[13] Beethoven also used the same *Prometheus*-theme in a set of ballroom dances he produced for the Viennese social season in the winter of 1801-02.[14] Many think (or assume) that the salon-music preceded the ballet (essentially, because it is in simpler form). If the theme originated from a straightforward monetary commission for a set of ballroom dances, it is difficult to see why Beethoven felt there were any "heroic" aspects to its character. Indeed, some musicologists have tried to deny Beethoven any originality in his Symphony whatsoever, by suggesting that he borrowed both the *Prometheus*-theme and the theme of his first movement from earlier works. Some argue that the latter, for example, must have been taken from Mozart's comic opera, *Bastien and Bastienne*:[15]

Fig. 1: W.A. Mozart, *Intrada* to *Bastien et Bastienne* (1768)

Another scholar claims to show that Beethoven borrowed the *Prometheus*-theme itself from Clementi:[16]

Fig. 2: Muzio Clementi, Sonata in G Minor, op. 7, No. 3, first movement, bars 102-09

Evidence from the Wielhorsky and other sketchbooks provides the key to demolishing these claims of borrowing. Instead of appearing from the outset in its final form, as though Beethoven had "remembered" it from some earlier work, the first-movement opening theme evolved in a linear progression that can be traced in the sketches, starting from the *Prometheus*-theme that Beethoven already planned to use in the Symphony finale. As for the latter theme, it emerged, as we shall see, from Beethoven's systematic depiction of the artistic growth experienced by "Prometheus' creatures" (*die Geschöpfe des Prometheus*) in the ballet.

The sketches for the E-flat symphony in the Wielhorsky sketchbook take up, as stated, only two pages near the front of the book. The next sketches for the symphony appear in the so-called *Eroica* sketchbook, which Beethoven began in the late spring of 1803, just as he was reaching the end of the Wielhorsky sketchbook.[17] They are much closer to the finished version. It is probable that there are interim loose-leaf sketches that are missing, but the only evidence we have indicates that Beethoven turned his attention away from his planned symphony after the fall of 1802, and did not resume work on it until the summer of 1803. If he was so inspired as to plan out the entire work after completing his sketches for opus 35, why did he then leave the project dormant for nearly nine months?

After he resumed work on the symphony in earnest, and it was near completion, Beethoven apparently formed an intention of dedicating the composition to Napoleon Bonaparte.[18] The story of his outburst upon learning that Napoleon had crowned himself Emperor, and of his furiously scratching out the symphony's inscription "intitolata Bonaparte" ("entitled Bonaparte"), is well known.[19] But what connection, if any, existed in Beethoven's mind between Prometheus and Napoleon? Who *was* the "hero" that Beethoven had in mind while he actually worked on the Third Symphony?

In this study, I shall use the evidence from the sketchbooks, from Beethoven's correspondence, and from contemporary accounts to offer answers to these questions. I will build on the ground laid by Fishman and others, as well as on an honors thesis I wrote in 1966.[20] The story to be told has often been surmised in part, and indicated in bits and pieces scattered here and there through the literature.[21] It will be the purpose of this study to try to bring them all together.

4

Chapter 2:
The Ballet Gli uomini di Prometeo (Die Geschöpfe des Prometheus)

In January 1801 Beethoven gave priority in his regimen to a new commission to write the music for a ballet to be presented at the Imperial Theater. We do not have the details of the commission, or of how the choice fell upon Beethoven to write the music. We do know, however, that the Empress herself, Marie Therese, had something to do with the matter, for that is how Beethoven himself reported it.[22] To understand her involvement, and its consequences for this ballet in particular, wc have to review the background of the ballet master, one Salvatore Viganò.

Plate 2: Salvatore Viganò

Viganò was born in Naples 21 months before Beethoven, in March 1769.[23]   His father was a noted choreographer and dancer; his mother was the sister of the composer Luigi Boccherini.   Viganò grew up dancing, playing the violin and learning the art of composition (evidently, however, without the help of his famous uncle, who by then resided permanently in Spain).[24] His debut as a ballet dancer came in 1783 when he was just fourteen; from then until 1788 he danced the female roles in his father's ballet company, since at that time women were not allowed on stage in Rome or Naples. At the age of nineteen he went to Madrid, where he took part in the coronation festivities for Charles IV and there met Jean Dauberval, an encounter which was to define his career. Dauberval was a well-respected French choreographer, and a follower of the principles of the "ballet d'action" as developed by the 18th-century ballet master Jean-Georges Noverre (for whose ballet *Les petits riens* no less than Mozart had written the music).[25] In Spain, too, Viganò met and married Josepha Maria Medina, a beautiful and highly talented ballet dancer who had made a successful transition from her native Vienna to Spain.[26] Dauberval took them with him to London, but the climate there was not conducive to their blood, and they returned to the Continent.

Plate 3: Maria Medina Viganò

Back in Italy, and working with his new wife in Venice (which did allow females to dance on stage), Viganò staged Dauberval's most celebrated creation, the comic action-ballet *La fille mal guardée,* which is still in the repertoire today. In 1793 the couple moved to Vienna, where they created a sensation by dancing a *pas de deux en rose*—exercising a

6

degree of freedom never before seen on the Viennese stage. (*See* Appendix B, p. 91.) Immediately Madame Viganò became the public's favorite, and Viennese fashions assiduously copied her costumes and hairstyles.[27] The ballets staged by her husband represented such a contrast with the static forms to which Vienna had been accustomed that the phrase began to circulate: "à la Viganò"—in the style of Viganò.[28]

Plate 4: Maria Viganò as Terpsichore

Viganò knew how to build on the publicity his beautiful wife was creating. In 1794 he presented the comic ballet *La fiera di Barcelona* ("The Fever of Barcelona"), in which the female dancers at one point appeared to be wearing nothing on stage, when in fact they were encased in flesh-colored body stockings. This created a scandal, and brought with it the censure of Cornelius van Ayrenhoff, an influential and distinguished military officer who had become a self-appointed *arbiter elegantiae* for Viennese society. The rebuke in turn led to a celebrated feud carried on in print and in the audiences over which was the better style of ballet: van Ayrenhoff was an admirer of the formalistic style of Antonio Muzzarelli, the long-standing ballet master for the Burgtheater, while Viganò, as we have seen, advocated the new style of plot and action introduced by Noverre and Dauberval.[29]

With his success at the court theater temporarily tarnished by van Ayrenhoff, Viganò took his company on tour through central Europe between 1795 and 1798. During this tour, tensions apparently mounted between Viganò and his beautiful wife. Rumors of her affairs had begun to circulate, along with the accounts of her great style and beauty, already while Maria Viganò danced on the stage in Vienna—some apparently connected her even with Kaiser Franz II.[30] At any rate, what we know is that in 1799 the Viganòs divorced, and Maria went back to Spain and a celebrated career, while Viganò returned to Vienna. In his company he brought with him a number of highly talented dancers and choreographers, including the brothers Gaetano and Ferdinando Gioja, the couple Filippo and Amalia Cesari, and a new solo ballerina, Maria Casentini (*see* Plate 5), whom Viganò hoped would find as much favor with the public as had his former wife.

It is a measure of the favor that Viganò enjoyed at the imperial court to note that, on his return in 1799, he was engaged as the dance director for the Burgtheater, with the obligation to produce at least one new original work each year.[31] This commission presumably left him free to engage the artists with whom he collaborated. It is against this background, therefore, that one must assess the decision by Viganò in late 1800 or early 1801 a) to stage for his third production a ballet on the subject of Prometheus, and

b) to engage Beethoven to compose its music.

For Viganò, it was an opportunity to ingratiate himself further with the Empress. His choice of Beethoven may have produced some resistance within the imperial bureaucracy, however, since no commission had ever gone before to that composer from the court of Franz II.[32] (Beethoven's republican sentiments were by 1800 well known in Vienna[33] and earned him no favors with the court, where the name of Napoleon was scorned and belittled.[34]) It was a defensible choice, nevertheless: here was a composer who had studied with Haydn, who was the author of a highly praised symphony, two piano concertos, six string quartets and a very popular septet, to say nothing of his works for solo piano.[35] He was already well connected with the leading noble families of Vienna, and was obviously a rising star. Had Viganò taken the trouble to inquire (and we do not know if he did), he would have learned about the young composer's already extensive experience with producing operas and ballets on the stage at Bonn, as well as his familiarity with the Vienna theaters.[36]

All the same, the decision to commission Beethoven seems to have been taken at the last minute, in some haste. The letter of Caspar Josef Eberl referred to earlier[37] shows that Beethoven appears to have recently adjusted his schedule to be able to work on the music, and it referred to March 1 as the date when Eberl learned about the commission from Beethoven. Since the ballet was originally scheduled to open on March 21, Beethoven was facing a deadline less than three weeks away.[38] It cannot be definitively decided whether the delay in engaging Beethoven was due to procrastination by Viganò, or by foot-dragging among palace bureaucrats once his name was put forward, but my suspicion is that it was the latter.

We do not have a scenario for the ballet that resulted, perhaps for the good reason that none ever formally existed.[39] From indications in Beethoven's sketches, as well as from the conflicts between the surviving sources, it appears that he and Viganò may have collaborated and exchanged ideas as the work progressed, without proceeding from any prescribed text, or "book". A present-day reconstruction of the ballet must base itself on the following sources:

- A public announcement (Plate 6) of the first performance (in which the work is called "Die Menschen des Prometheus", or "The Men of Prometheus");[40]

Plate 6: *Prometheus* circular

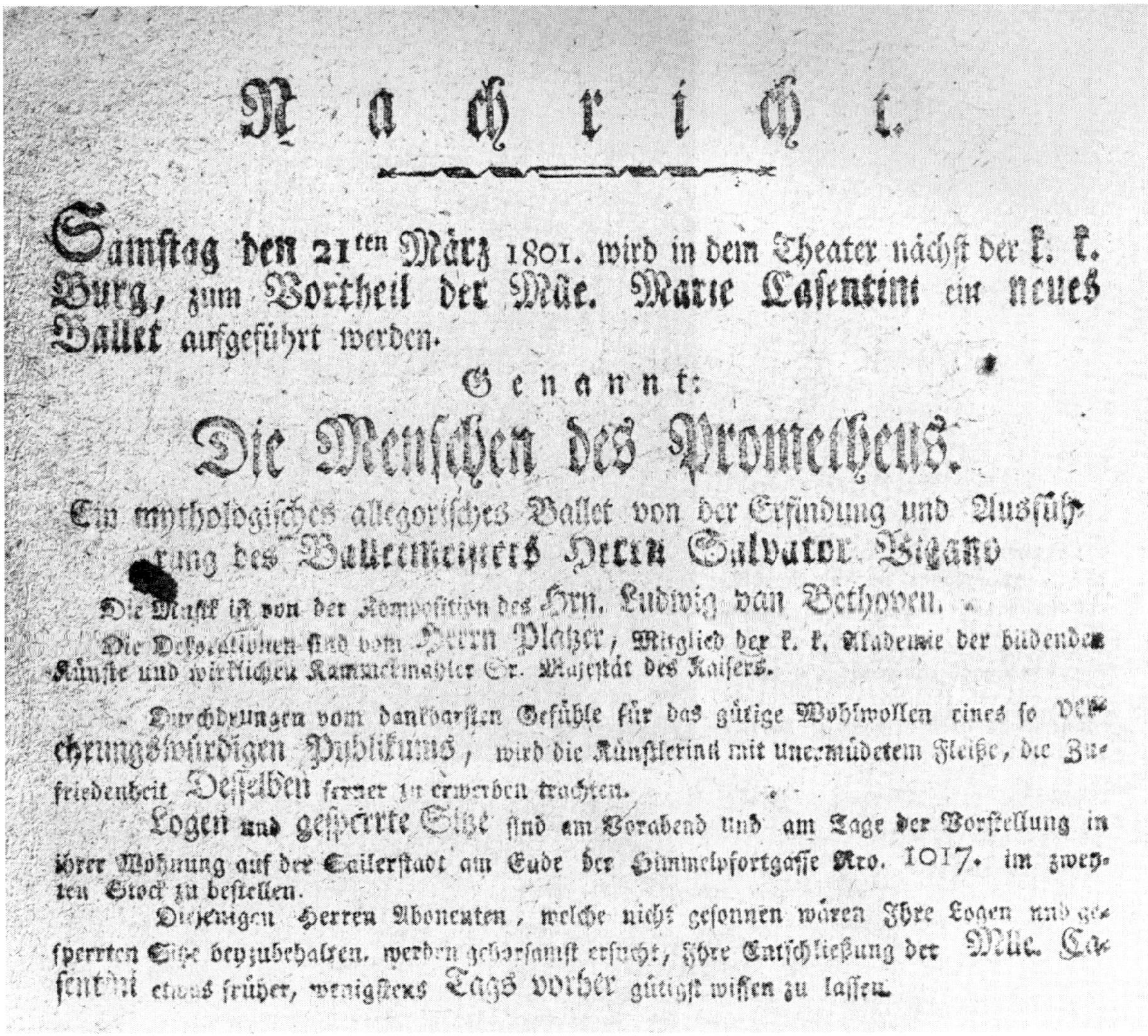

Nachricht.

Samstag den 21ten März 1801. wird in dem Theater nächst der k. k. Burg, zum Vortheil der Mlle. Marie Casentini ein neues Ballet aufgeführt werden.

Genannt:

Die Menschen des Prometheus.

Ein mythologisches allegorisches Ballet von der Erfindung und Ausführung des Balletmeisters Herrn Salvator Vigano.

Die Musik ist von der Komposition des Hrn. Ludwig van Bethoven.

Die Dekorationen sind vom Herrn Platzer, Mitglied der k. k. Akademie der bildenden Künste und wirklichen Kammermahler Sr. Majestät des Kaisers.

Durchdrungen vom dankbarsten Gefühle für das gütige Wohlwollen eines so verehrungswürdigen Publikums, wird die Künstlerinn mit unermüdetem Fleiße, die Zufriedenheit Desselben ferner zu erwerben trachten.

Logen und gesperrte Sitze sind am Vorabend und am Tage der Vorstellung in ihrer Wohnung auf der Sailerstadt am Ende der Himmelpfortgasse Nro. 1017. im zweyten Stock zu bestellen.

Diejenigen Herren Abonenten, welche nicht gesonnen wären Ihre Logen und gesperrten Sitze beyzubehalten, werden gehorsamst ersucht, Ihre Entschließung der Mlle. Casentini etwas früher, wenigstens Tags vorher gütigst wissen zu lassen.

- A playbill (Plate 7) preserved from that opening performance, which gives only a summary of the action (that conflicts in part with the next source);[41]

Plate 7: *Prometheus* playbill

- An account of and commentary on the ballet's scenes (chiefly the first nine only), compiled (perhaps long afterward) by Viganò's biographer, Carlo Ritorni, and not published until 1838, seventeen years after Viganò's death in Milan;[42]

- Beethoven's surviving sketches for the work, in the "Landsberg 7" sketchbook (transcribed and published by Karl Mikulicz [Mikulicz (ed.) 1927]);

- A handwritten orchestral score used at the early performances, with annotations and revisions in Beethoven's hand (as well as in other hands), preserved in the Austrian National Library (this will be referred to as a "working score");

- Contemporary newspaper accounts of the performance;[43] and

- A surviving letter from Beethoven to his publisher, in which he expresses his satisfaction with the music he wrote, but reports that the "ballet master did not do his job all that well"[44].

To this list may be added some secondary sources, such as the accounts that survive of a much-expanded version of the ballet that was choreographed and performed by Viganò in Milan in 1813.[45]

The title page to the orchestral working score in the Austrian National Library reads as follows:

Coppia corretta dall' Autore

Proprietà del Negozio – Artaria & Com.

Ballo serio

Die Geschöpfe des Prometheus

Composta di

Sign. Luigi van Beethoven

After the overture, the score for the first number repeats the title, but in Italian: "*Gli uomini di Prometeo / Balletto / di Beethoven*". Thus the change from "Menschen" to "Geschöpfe" in the German title was not a change of substance, but, as noted, was probably done for marketing purposes (nn. 12 and 40).

The first thing to note is that the work is self-described as a *ballo serio*. This contrasts with the description given by the playbill (Plate 7) for the first performance: "Ein Heroisches, allegorisches Ballet . . .." (The announcement [Plate 6], on the other hand, describes the ballet using the terms "Ein mythisches, allegorisches Ballet . . ." while the piano score, published in 1801, uses only the word "Ballo", standing alone.[46]) Was there any difference intended between the descriptions, as of 1801, of an "heroic-allegoric", "mythic-allegoric", and a "serious" ballet? It does not seem likely. The category "*ballo serio*" identifies with the genre of operas based on the classical themes from ancient tragedy, the *opera seria*; and such operas could also be described as "heroic" or "mythic" if they drew upon figures from Greek or Roman mythology or epics.[47] There would obviously be much room for overlap, since nearly all classical tragedy used heroic characters.

The term "allegoric", however, calls for more elaboration. By this term, Viganò intended to convey that his ballet presented an allegory—but of what? The action, so to speak, consists solely of human clay figures being brought to life and taught how to reason, dance and make music. The allegory, therefore, lies in the progressive development of the human race through the arts—this is one level. But there is a second level, far more specific to the circumstances: the Empress as the representative of the Imperial Court had commissioned the ballet. The entire second act of the ballet takes place at the heavenly court of Apollo, where the humans are instructed in the various arts. Thus the court of Apollo is an allegory for the Hapsburg court, which is represented as host and sponsor to all the arts, but foremost to those of dance and music.

These two levels of allegory operate in different planes. The former is more abstract and idealistic, the latter highly concrete and specific. Is it to be wondered, then, that the composer was much more drawn to the former, while the choreographer was oriented almost exclusively to the latter? And as we shall see, just as each saw their joint creation in different terms, so each used the work as a springboard to highly different ends.

Historians of the dance are understandably rather upset when they read pieces by musicologists which attempt to equate the allegorical Titan of the 1801 ballet with the human figure of Napoleon.[48] After all, anyone familiar with the Imperial Court and the commissioning of the ballet should see that the last work that Marie Therese would expect to result from her behest would be an allegorical tribute to her husband's archenemy.[49] It may be equally upsetting to those same musicologists to read that the

14

ballet, far from being considered by dance historians as an example of a *ballo eroico* (and hence supporting their construct of an allegory portraying Napoleon), is treated as but another in a long tradition of eighteenth-century entertainments presented to glorify and reflect the majesty and enlightened character of the imperial court. Usually consisting of two parts, they opened with a *Prolog* that set the scene and then followed with a *Divertissement* ("entertainment") that through costume, scenery and machinery presented a series of varied scenes meant to divert, surprise and entertain the assembled audience.[50]

The differing viewpoints of the terpsichologists and the musicologists stem from the differing levels of allegory mentioned earlier. Viganò, given a commission by the court for a ballet to be presented in the Imperial Theater, resorted to a traditional form of courtly entertainment that would afford him the maximum opportunity to show off different styles of dance, as interpreted by distinguished members of his own company, not the least of whom was himself. At the same time, he was careful to choose an allegorical subject that would furnish both a dramatic prologue as well as a means to glorify the Imperial court.

For his part, Beethoven was no stranger to dance music, or courtly entertainments.[51] He was less interested in glorifying the Imperial court, however, since as a republican he could accept a court appointment only if it were offered to him in acknowledgment of his merit. This meant that the occasion called for his best possible work. If the sovereign chose to recognize and reward its merit, then so much the better did such a recognition reflect back on the intelligence of the sovereign, and so much the worse for the sovereign if he proved incapable of recognizing the worth of what had been offered.

Beethoven did not let the court commission constrain the kind of music he wrote, but let the music be determined by the subject matter, by the allegory itself. And on the higher plane of the allegory—on its more abstract and idealized level, in depicting the cultural progress of mankind through music and the arts—Beethoven found all the inspiration he required.

The subject, after all, was a figure already well known to Beethoven, with his classical education and his enduring love for noble themes.[52] It was that of the fire-giver, Prometheus, the Titan who steals a heavenly spark from the forge of Vulcan and brings it to earth for the benefit of mankind.[53] In the version of the myth elaborated by Viganò, Prometheus uses the divine spark to enkindle life into two figures—one a man, the other a woman—that he has previously fashioned from clay. To his great delight, the figures come gradually to life, with awkward, jerky movements. But then Prometheus sees that they lack all the higher faculties of reason and esthetic appreciation. At first he grows angry, and momentarily considers destroying his creations. With a sudden inspiration, however, he leads them off to the court of Apollo, on Mount Parnassus.

15

Up to this point the action is the prologue (Act I in the score), enlivened by a storm in which Zeus hurls his thunderbolts after Prometheus as he runs to earth with the heavenly fire.[54] With the arrival of the humans on Parnassus, however, the *divertissement propre* commences. Apollo summons the Muses, Bacchus, Pan, Orpheus, and (somewhat anachronistically, as Ritorni wryly comments) the yet-to-be-born Arion and Amphion, to instruct the humans in the various arts.[55] This is Act II of the score, in which dance follows dance, of the most varied sort, from shepherd's dance to military march to a dance of fauns and satyrs, grotesquely leaping, until the all-inclusive finale signifying the culmination of the humans' cultural progress, where they join in dance with the gods themselves.

The allegory by which Viganò intended to glorify the court of the Hapsburgs is patently clear. For Beethoven, however, the matter was not so simple. As the title makes clear, Prometheus is not the focus of the piece either as choreographed or composed. Other than the pieces in Act I, Beethoven wrote no music specifically for Prometheus; Viganò chose the part of the created man as his own to dance, rather than the role of the Titan (*see* Plate 7, p. 12). Nevertheless, as we shall see, for Beethoven the music he composed, especially the final number, became inextricably bound to the *heroic ideal* of Prometheus. This ideal transcends Viganò's particular Enlightenment-bound scenario, and relates back to the classical figure in Greek mythology. In that myth, there were three key elements, one of which we have touched upon already—Prometheus as the gift-giver, or bringer to man of the essence of life. The other two elements have gone unmentioned until now, because of the particular treatment given to them by Viganò. The first is the element of Prometheus as having been *unjustly punished* by the gods for his act of giving to the human race. The second, and equally important, element is the fact of Prometheus' *refusal to succumb to that punishment, i.e.,* his *enduring* and *surviving* a punishment that was unjustly imposed.[56]

In classical mythology, Zeus had Prometheus chained to a rock with divinely strengthened links fashioned by Vulcan. Each day an eagle flew down to gnaw out Prometheus' liver, and each night, the immortal Titan regenerated himself, only to suffer the same torture again and again, until the demigod Hercules (sired by Zeus) broke his chains as one of his assigned labors. In the ballet, Viganò does not have Prometheus suffer such a fate. In a scene that may have caused some astonishment to the Viennese nobility, and which is severely criticized by Viganò's biographer Ritorni, Viganò has the Titan first accused in front of his creatures by the Muse of tragedy, Melpomene, of bringing humans to life with no purpose other than to see them suffer and die as mortals. Then, supposedly to illustrate to the poor creatures her point, she draws a dagger and stabs Prometheus in the chest, causing him to slump to the ground as if dead. (It was the death of a man onstage at the hand of a woman that called forth Ritorni's criticism, and that may have shocked the nobility as well, if indeed it was played on stage as Ritorni describes it. It may have been this reaction to which Beethoven referred obliquely in the letter cited above.[57])

In analogy to the myth, where Prometheus as an immortal Titan cannot die or be killed, Viganò uses a subsequent dance (probably the "solo di Gioja", or dance of Bacchus, but the details are conflicting and unclear) to revive Prometheus, to the ensuing joy of his creatures, each of whom dances a solo themselves. The ballet then closes with a general *finale* in rondo form, in which the so-called "*Prometheus*-theme", or "*Prometheus*-melody", returns again and again, interspersed with other short dances.

In each case, in both the myth's classical version and in the treatment given to it by Viganò, the punishment meted out to Prometheus is seen (from the human point of view) as unjust. Although many have commented on Beethoven's possible identification with the myth of Prometheus,[58] and have traced musical and programmatic connections between Beethoven's ballet and subsequent compositions (chiefly the *Eroica* symphony),[59] none has given sufficient weight, I think, to the impetus provided to Beethoven by these key second and third elements of the core Prometheus-myth.[60] For as his letters make clear, Beethoven also saw his impending deafness as a kind of punishment—a particularly harsh punishment for one who made his living by playing and composing music—*that was unjustly imposed, and that notwithstanding, was to be endured—and survived—by the victim.*[61] It was easy for Beethoven to identify with the gift-giving aspect of Prometheus, and to feel nobly inspired to bestow upon man music that sprang, like Vulcan's fire, from some divine source. Much harder it was to take the cup of unjust punishment that went with the role of gift-giver, and to drink it to the dregs. It was surely the example of Prometheus' response to his unjustly imposed suffering that gave Beethoven the strength to endure his deafness, and to surmount it—in the process, enabling him to identify with the third element of the classical myth. And it is in appreciating this key point, I submit, that we can begin to understand why the music he wrote for the ballet *Prometheus* took on such importance for Beethoven, for his subsequent compositional breakthroughs, and for the history of music itself.

Although Goethe published a remarkable poem on Prometheus in 1773,[62] of which Beethoven was almost certainly cognizant, I submit that it is the English poet and contemporary of Beethoven, Percy Bysshe Shelley, who has expressed in verse what the ideal of Prometheus represented for romantics of the day. At the end of his *Prometheus Unbound*, he set out the Titan's credo:[63]

17

To suffer woes which Hope thinks infinite;
To forgive wrongs darker than death or night;
    To defy Power, which seems omnipotent;
To love, and bear; to hope till Hope creates
From its own wreck the thing it contemplates;
    Neither to change, nor falter, nor repent;
This, like thy glory, Titan, is to be
Good, great and joyous, beautiful and free;
This is alone Life, Joy, Empire and Victory.

In his Heiligenstadt Testament and in a few of the letters written in these same crucial years, Beethoven showed his deep sense of identity with this ideal.[64] But it is in his works of this same period that his resonance with the suffering hero-figure is most evident: Prometheus in the ballet, Jesus in the Garden of Gethsemane in *Christus am Oelberge*, Florestan in *Fidelio*: all share themes of suffering (and forgiving) unjust wrongs, of defiance of power and authority, and of endurance till the hero is redeemed through love.[65] What is unique about the ballet is that it came first in this sequence, as Beethoven was just beginning to surmount his deafness. We shall begin by examining its music more closely, in order to understand how its evolution within the work is key to understanding the evolution of the subsequent works (a rough equivalent, in the musical sphere, to what "ontogeny recapitulates phylogeny" expresses in the biological sphere). Once we have completed that task, we will be in a better position to appreciate how Beethoven's creation of the *Eroica* may indeed be viewed as the result of "hop[ing] till Hope creates / From its own wreck the thing it contemplates."

Chapter 3:
The Music of the Ballet

Beethoven's *The Creatures of Prometheus*, composed in 1801 and published in a piano reduction in 1802, stands as the only independent ballet score produced by a major composer of the nineteenth century until Tchaikovsky composed *Swan Lake* in 1875. With the possible exception of its Overture, Beethoven's music for *Prometheus* has been quite neglected. Whether this is the fault of the scenario or of posterity need not detain us; we must, however, examine the music in detail if we wish to trace the subsequent uses which the composer made of it.

The ballet enjoyed a successful run of 14 performances in 1801 and nine more in 1802, but then was not performed again until 1843.[66] A summary of the work through the first nine numbers is given in a now rare biography of Viganò written by Carlo Ritorni and published in 1838, seventeen years after Viganò's death.[67] Ritorni is vague, however, in his description of the action in the last seven numbers of the ballet, and the surviving sketches are equally silent. What little we can know about the final numbers comes from the headings in the working score, and from the contemporary accounts, including a review of the opening night. Published in *Zeitung für die elegante Welt* I (April 1801), at 485-87, it is significant for noting how far Beethoven's music, in the critic's view, had departed from the function which Viganò intended of providing an entertaining *divertissement*:

"The presentations at our court theater before Easter concluded with a new heroic-allegorical ballet in two acts: *Die Geschöpfe des Prometheus*, invented and developed by Mr. *Salvatore Viganò* and set to music by Mr. *van Beethoven*. The first time, it was given for the benefit of the famous dancer, Miss *Casentini*. Its content was announced in a very peculiar program, presumably written by an Italian not very well versed in the German language.

"Prometheus rescues the people of his time from their ignorance, improves them with knowledge and art, and elevates them to moral awareness. This is the subject in brief. As much dignity and artistic design as it had, and as masterfully as some dancers, most notably Mr. Viganò himself, distinguished themselves, it nevertheless was not liked in general. The least satisfying of all to our spectacle-loving public was the fact that the stage remained completely unchanged from the second scene of the first act until the very end. The action began with a thunderstorm. The theater presented a small grove in which there were two children of Prometheus. Suddenly their father entered with a burning torch. (Where, and with what fire he lighted it, the spectators did not get to see.) After he had placed the fire on the breast of each child, they began at once to toddle around stiffly without gesticulating. (This scene lasted rather too long and became boring.) Now Prometheus led them to Apollo. Parnassus with all its dwellers did not exactly make the most agreeable sight. The nine Muses remained like lifeless statues upon their assigned spot until it was their turn to dance, and Apollo himself sat upon the highest peak of the mountain, always motionless. Perhaps this very scene made too little impression upon the artistic spirit of our beloved *Casentini,* for she, introduced by her father to the god of the muses, expressed no interest at all and, with conspicuous indifference, immediately allowed her glance to wander to other things. One can certainly not convince oneself that she should have ignored the respect she owes to such a public, particularly in a ballet that brought her over 4,000 gulden in receipts, simply because of a bad mood. Assuredly, however, with just a little more effort—even though a *Casentini* can never dance poorly—she would have made the ballet much more attractive.

"The music also did not entirely live up to expectations, even though it possesses more than *ordinary* merit. Whether Mr. *van Beethoven* can achieve what a public like ours demands in regard to unity—which is not to say uniformity—of treatment, I will leave undecided. However, that he wrote *too learnedly* for a ballet, and with too little regard for the dance, is certainly not subject to doubt. Everything is laid out too grandly for a diversion, which is what the ballet should actually be, and because of the lack of suitable situations, it had to remain more of a fragment than a whole. This begins already with the overture. In any more substantial opera, it would be in the proper place and would not fail to make a significant effect. Here, however, it is in the wrong place. The warlike dances and Miss *Casentini's* solo, on the other hand, were probably the most successful for the composer. In the *Dance of Pan,* some people claim to find various reminiscences from other ballets. However, it seems to me that this is doing Mr. van B. a disservice, especially since only those who envy him can deny him his totally extraordinary originality, through which he admittedly often denies his observers the charm of sweetly pleasing harmonies."[68]

A musical analysis of the ballet cannot fail to take note of the Overture, which contains no musical elements directly related to the rest of the work. It is an independent unit, and at the same time a highly successful curtain-raiser; it was frequently performed in Beethoven's day. (Said one reviewer in 1826, a quarter century after the ballet's premiere: "...Beethoven's overture to the ballet *Prometheus*...was undoubtedly performed for the ninety-ninth time on today's concert, as if, as it were, no other overture existed for this purpose. When 'Overture' or even 'Overture by Beethoven' is on the concert program, one can wager a hundred to one that the above-mentioned, and no other, will be played. It is very beautiful, but heard much, much too often."[69]) Some (including Nathan

Fishman) claim to recognize in its strong, fortissimo thrusts a portrayal of the resoluteness of the ballet's title figure, who is the first to appear on stage after the curtain goes up.[70]

Following the overture there is an unnumbered "Introduzione" (*Allegro non troppo*, 4/4), which in the piano score is further designated "*La Tempesta*".[71] Zeus has raised the fierce storm depicted here in his wrath at Prometheus, who has dared to steal celestial fire from Vulcan's forge and has run away with it to the earth. The choreographic action begins as the hero, who has managed to elude Zeus's thunderbolts, appears onstage with a burning torch, and approaches what appear to be clay statues of a man and a woman. At the Introduction's end, two *forte* chords accompany the dramatic kindling of the statues' hearts with the divine fire. The orchestra subsides to *piano*, over the soft *tremolo* of the tympani—Prometheus, exhausted, awaits the result of his deed.

Short, hesitant *piano* chords in the strings open the ballet's first number: the creatures come to life and take their first steps. Their awkward movements are described in the jerky rhythm of the eighth-note chords set off by rests of varying length:

Fig. 3: *Die Geschöpfe des Prometheus,* op. 43, No. 1 (Poco Adagio)

Prometheus observes, enthralled—then breaks into an outburst of joy: *Allegro con brio.* The graceful turns, leaps and trills of his music are in sharp contrast to the broken notes that portray the creatures' clumsy steps.

Fig. 4: *Die Geschöpfe des Prometheus,* op. 43, No. 1 (*Allegro con brio*)

That this contrast was intended by Beethoven to denote the movement of the god as opposed to the movement of the creatures, there can be no doubt: on pages 73-75 of the Landsberg 7 sketchbook, he has written above his draft of this scene a bar-by-bar account of the action depicted in the music. Each time the chords in separated eighth notes occur, Beethoven's commentary is referring to the motions of the humans, while the words describing Prometheus' actions always appear above the arpeggios and running passages in sixteenth notes (given mostly to the first violins in the score).

The human beings are not yet capable of thought or emotion, however; they remain insensitive to the gift Prometheus has given them. In the second and third numbers Prometheus becomes alternately piteous of and angry with them—at one point he is dissuaded from his intent to destroy them only by a voice from on high that speaks to him inwardly. Finally he decides to bring them to the temple of Apollo on Mount Parnassus, where they can receive education in the arts. This resolve fires him with hope, and the first act closes with an exuberant coda to the third number.

The court of Phoebus Apollo on Mount Parnassus is the setting of the second act of the ballet, designed by Viganò as a vehicle for a series of diverse entertainments. Powerful D-major chords, *Maestoso*, delineate the splendor and majesty of the scene. (According to Ritorni, Viganò had the novel idea of letting the curtain first rise on the set without either accompanying action or music, so that the audience would gain the maximum impression from the spectacle before its eyes.[72] Beethoven's regal music then underscored the visual effect of the scene—which, however, failed to impress the opening

24

night reviewer.[73]) Then, once more, the broken eighth-note chords: Prometheus leads in the two humans and requests that Apollo acquaint them with the art and skill of the gods in music and dance.

The fifth number opens with harp arpeggios, one of the extremely rare instances of the use of that instrument in a Beethoven score. It sets the level for what is to follow, and represents the divine musician, Apollo himself, summoning celestial tones from his lyre. In the beautiful music that ensues, the creatures are serenaded first by Euterpe, the muse of lyric poetry, accompanied by Amphion (flute solo), and then by Orpheus with Arion (violoncello solo). Terpsichore, muse of the dance, performs a graceful ballet in triple time for them. Then the merry Bacchus and his attendants, together with the armed companions of the god of war, Mars, excite the creatures with a "heroic dance" meant to awake in them a desire for deeds of valor. This design succeeds, as toward the end of the eighth number the creatures take up weapons and join the group in a martial scene that must have resonated with those who were concerned about Napoleon's advancing armies.

Suddenly the muse of tragedy, Melpomene, enters. She stages a dance revealing to the humans their inevitable destiny—the end of life in death. The creatures are filled with terror and horror. Melpomene flings an accusation at Prometheus: why has he created these unfortunate beings and given birth to such suffering?

The orchestra crescendos depict the sentence pronounced by Melpomene: Prometheus himself must die. There follows a series of *sforzando* chords—on the last one, Melpomene strikes him with her dagger, and he falls to the ground. The man and the woman are stunned. They react in dazed confusion, and finally they sink, weeping, by their fallen benefactor.

This was the scene that aroused the critics' indignation at Viganò. They could not accept the hero's violent death taking place on stage – at the hands of a woman.[74] For his part, Beethoven seems to have subscribed fully to the concept. In his sketches he marked the appropriate passages "Prom: weint", "Promethe mort", "les enfants pleurent", "Vorwürfe dem Prometheus", "va in collera", and once again, "Promet: mort" (*see* pp. 109-111 of Landsberg 7). Like the final version, these sketches are all in C minor, and various commentators, including Fishman, Floros, and Maruyama, have pointed out how some of the sketches bear resemblance to passages from the funeral march of the *Eroica* Symphony.[75]

Indeed, in the midst of the sketches just referred to, on page 110 of Landsberg 7, Beethoven has inscribed above a staff the word "Sinfonia", beneath which is a sketch in C minor for what is unquestionably a funeral march.

Fig. 5: Landsberg 7 Sketchbook (tr. K. Mikulicz, 1927), p. 110, lines 5-7

Fishman draws attention to the similarity of its concluding phrase to an 1803 sketch for the *Eroica's Marcia funebre*, as transcribed by Gustav Nottebohm:[76]

Fig. 6: 1801 sketch for Op. 43, No. 9 compared with 1803 sketch for Op. 55/2

One could as easily compare two passages from the finished works: the coda at the end of the ninth number of the ballet and the coda at the end of the *Maggiore* section of the funeral march in the Third Symphony (bars 101-104):

Fig. 7: Op. 43, No. 9 (*Coda*) compared to Op. 55/2, 101-104

26

This evidence, standing alone, may be insufficient to sustain any conjecture about the connections between Prometheus' death music and the second movement of the Third Symphony. It is, however, worth noting the degree to which, according to the evidence of the sketches, funeral music for a fallen hero was occupying Beethoven's mind at this time: sketches for the third movement of the piano sonata op. 26—the movement entitled *"Marcia funebre sulla morte d'un eroe"* —both precede and follow in Landsberg 7 the Prometheus death scene sketches described above.

The tenth number of the ballet is a "Pastorale". By combining Ritorni's abbreviated account with the program notes, one can surmise that this was the "Schäfertanz" ("sheep dance") mentioned in the latter, the invention of Pan who leads it with his pipes, during which Thalia, the comic muse, dances with her masks in front of the humans to show them that Prometheus' death was not real, but only staged. The short, introductory eleventh number and the more elaborate one that follows are designated in the working score "Coro di Gioja" and "Solo di Gioja", respectively. Since Ferdinando Gioja danced the role of Bacchus, we can assume that the short No. 11 served to usher on stage his suite of Bacchantes, followed by his dramatic solo entrance and ensuing dance (No. 12), during which he (or perhaps Pan, at his bidding—*see* Ritorni, Appendix C, p. 96) summons Prometheus to arise.

In keeping with the idea of successive "entertainments", there now follows No. 13 of the ballet, entitled in the working score "*Grot[t]eschi Terzettino*" (little trio of grotesques). The sketches for this number indicate that it consisted of three short solo dances for two men and a woman, interspersed with passages for a group of dancers. In his monograph on the ballet, German musicologist Constantin Floros suggests that this was a type of ballet known at the time (and considered one of its lowest forms) in which peasant types leapt and cavorted grotesquely about, heedless of meter and form.[77]

The buildup to the climax of the ballet begins with No. 14, the "*Solo della Sig^(ra) Casentini*", which is specified as following without pause the *danse grotesque*. Maria Casentini was the dancer who replaced Viganò's former wife as his company's female lead; in *Prometheus* she danced the part of the female brought to life by the Titan. As noted, the opening night's performance of *Prometheus* was held for her benefit—presumably to allow her to establish herself in the imperial capital and begin to build a following, as had Madame Viganò.[78]

In any event, the music of No. 14 consists of an evocative introduction, followed by a languorous *Adagio* in which Beethoven pairs an oboe with a basset horn—the only instance of this instrument in a Beethoven score. What appears to be portrayed is an awakening of the emotion of love, in which the choreography probably called on Signora Casentini to attempt a little seduction on her male counterpart. The number ends with a sprightly *Allegro/Allegretto,* 2/4, which could not present a stronger contrast with the halting chords that accompanied Signora Casentini's first attempts at movement.

The same striking contrast appears in No. 15, a solo for the male figure, danced by Viganò himself. There is an opening flourish as he takes his position, followed by an *Adagio* in 2/4 in which he responds to the emotions displayed by his partner. (This time the duet is between the clarinet and the bassoon.) As with No. 14, Beethoven then gives him a lively closing *Allegro* in which to show off all his newfound abilities, and which, as befits the ballet master, is significantly longer and more elaborate than the music for the preceding solo.

And so we come to the finale, No. 16. This is titled simply "Finale" in the working score; with Bacchus, Pan and the two human figures having danced their solos, is this then the occasion for a closing solo from the ballet's title figure? Nothing would so indicate. The movement is built in rondo form, and the repeated appearances of the celebrated theme are marked in the working score simply as "Thema", "Tema", *etc.* From Ritorni's brief description,[79] *"e così fra danze festive termina la favola"* ("and thus the story concludes amid festive dances"), as well as from the general practice in such *divertissements*, it is most likely that the concluding number furnished an occasion for all of the ballet's principal characters to dance together.

Such an interpretation of the Finale also makes dramatic sense. The fact that it is the human creatures who take over the action at the end of the ballet is significant—in terms of the plot, they have now attained maturity and are capable of experiencing joy and sorrow, love and heroism, as well as showing the capacity to learn from all their experiences. How appropriate it is, then, for the music to summarize this evolution. The last three numbers represent musically a development of the initial *Poco adagio* of the ballet's first number, a compositional feat that parallels the dramatic developments being shown on the stage. Gone are the broken and incomplete lines of the music first used to depict the creatures, just as awkwardness is now absent from their dancing:

Fig. 8: *Die Geschöpfe des Prometheus*, op. 43: Solo della Sig^ra Casentini (No. 14); Solo di Viganò (No. 15)

The culmination of this process, however—the most flowing and graceful of melodies—is reserved for the finale, when the two humans join the gods in a celebratory dance: it is the *"Prometheus* theme," the apotheosis of the musical and dramatic development that has occurred in the ballet:

Fig. 9: *Prometheus*-theme, Op. 43, No. 16 (*finale*).

Hugo Riemann saw this intuitively when he wrote: "Neither Apollo, nor any of the Muses, nor Bacchus, nor Pan, nor Amphion, nor Orpheus, but the two humans, having been brought to the peak of their development, are the heroes represented in the music."[80]

Riemann, however—and Fishman following him—did not pursue this insight far enough. For while it certainly is true that the outstanding progress in music and the arts made by the humans is embodied in the music of the finale, it is equally important *that the gods are seen as admitting the humans into their society, by dancing together with them at the end.* It is just this particular development that we know would resonate most with Beethoven's fierce egalitarianism, in which he saw himself, and kindred artists such as Goethe, as fully the equal of any nobility happening to walk the earth, whose advantages he saw as stemming solely from an accident of birth.[81] The rondo theme of the finale, in addition to expressing Prometheus' joy at the success of his creations, and the humans' delight in their new accomplishments, embodies the entire ideal that with proper instruction and inspiration, the human spirit can soar to heights at which mankind is able to consort with the gods themselves. And it is precisely in *this* high-principled context, I suggest—the spiritual evolution of the human race to a divine level, enacted through a musical allegory—that one must understand Beethoven's decision to give this theme a special place in his compositions.

Chapter 4:
Which Came First – Contredanse or Ballet?

The preceding analysis hinges on a central point: that the *"Prometheus* theme" is the result of a process of musical development that begins in the ballet's first number. It is essential, therefore, that one examine the relation of Beethoven's Contredanse No. 7 (WoO 14) to the finale of the ballet, because a large number of authorities, both current as well as nineteenth-century scholars, hold that the latter work was written before the ballet.[82] If that is indeed so, then the theme as first conceived did not possess the significance which we have attached to it: Beethoven would have thought of it first as a pretty dance tune, and considered it pretty enough to serve as a rondo theme in the ballet's final number.

As is the case with many scholarly Beethoven controversies, the source of this dispute may be laid at the feet of Anton Schindler, Beethoven's much-discredited biographer. Although he did not make Beethoven's acquaintance until 1814, in the third edition of his biography of the composer published in 1860 he wrote:[83]

"...one aspect [of the *Eroica* Symphony] that particularly incensed its scores of enemies was the melody in the fourth movement:

which was still familiar from its occurrence in the finale of the *Prometheus* ballet music. Those who condemned the symphony asked how one melody could be a dance in one place and the commemoration of a hero in another. This melody had been used much earlier in a collection of contredanses . . .".[84]

In fact, however, the "collection of contredanses" had been assembled by Beethoven for use during the winter ball season of 1801-1802; since he rarely wrote occasional music without a particular occasion in mind, they were probably compiled shortly before the first balls in the *Redoutensaal* took place in November 1801. The premiere of *Prometheus* took place some seven months earlier, on March 28, 1801. On what basis, then, can anyone reasonably assert that the composition of the contredanse preceded that of the ballet?

Schindler does not justify his assertion, but as in many other instances in which he has been discredited, simply puts it out as a fact. No contemporary criticism of the *Eroica* has been found which finds fault with the source of the theme for its finale, or which even mentions its connection to the ballet or the contredanse.[85]

One year before Schindler's third edition appeared, the German scholar Adolph Bernhard Marx published his own version of Beethoven's biography (Marx 1859). At page 212 of vol. I, Marx notes that the theme of the ballet, the piano variations and the symphony finale are all the same, but he makes no mention of the contredanse. This is the reason that we can be fairly certain that the idea the contredanse came first originated with Schindler in 1860.[86] Its intuitive appeal depends on the notion that the simpler must precede the more complex—that Beethoven would be more likely to adapt an earlier dance tune to special purposes than he would be to take a tune he had developed for special purposes and use it as a casual dance piece. In other words, the linear progression of simple dance tune – ballet finale – variations theme – symphony finale is more logical than trying to account for how the dance came to be written between the ballet and the variations. Nevertheless, as we shall see, and as Justice Holmes once wrote in an entirely different context, "Upon this point a page of history is worth a volume of logic."[87]

Marx's biography was subjected to a devastating critique by Alexander Wheelock Thayer in which Thayer accused Marx of blindly perpetuating Schindler's numerous errors and inaccuracies.[88] It is therefore remarkable to see how Thayer, careful as he was, fell into his own errors concerning the sequence of the four works, and how his successors, in trying to improve on what he did, made still more. To begin with, Thayer had cautiously explored the question in the first German edition of his life of Beethoven, published in 1872[89] (from notes made much earlier, and based on his reading of Wilhelm von Lenz's description, published in 1860, of the contents of the Wielhorsky sketchbook):[90]

"Is it possible that Court Councilor Lenz confused studies for the piano variations Op. 35 with those for the finale of the *Eroica*? If not, then this sketchbook offers us a very interesting clarification: that in the spring [of 1801] Beethoven worked the *Prometheus*-theme into a set of variations for orchestra; that in autumn he changed his mind and used the same sketches in the piano variations; that in the winter he transformed the theme into a contredanse (perhaps to make it more well-known?), and finally in 1803 he returned to his original idea of the *Sinfonia Eroica* and elaborated the orchestral variations as the finale, while the funeral march [also described by von Lenz as among the sketches], took the place of the slow movement."[91]

Thayer suspected that von Lenz had misread the sketches, but took the latter's description at face value and used it to construct an erroneous chronology. It is thus ironic to have to note that while the part that Thayer based on von Lenz's mistaken reading of the sketches was quickly corrected by Ludwig Nohl in 1874, the part that he got right—that the ballet preceded the composition of the contredanse—was afterwards changed by Thayer's subsequent editors. Hermann Deiters, who translated and edited the German edition of Thayer's biography, and who following Thayer's death worked on completing it until he himself died in 1907, was the first to offer a justification in print for concluding that the contredanse must have come before the ballet.[92] Deiters simply compared the published scores of the two works, and noted that the octave leap in the opening bars of the bass, which Beethoven made the subject of several variations in op. 35 and also in the Third Symphony, is present in the ballet, but not in the contredanse. He reasoned that since the octave leap was so fundamental (*wichtig*) to Beethoven's integrated concept of the theme, the simpler version of the contredanse must have preceded it:[93]

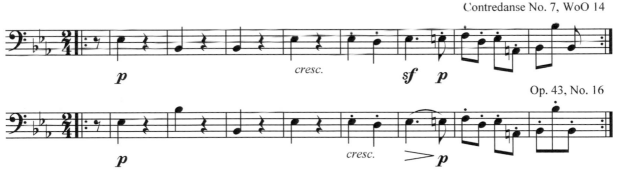

Fig. 10: Bass line of Contredanse WoO 14, No, 7 compared with bass line of Op. 43, No. 16

Such reasoning, however, is anachronistic. The first time that Beethoven showed any interest in treating the bass line of the theme as a variation subject in its own right was not in the ballet music, but in the *Prometheus* variations for piano, op. 35, which were composed *after* both the ballet and the contredanse.[94] Consequently, the assertion that the octave leap in the bass is "fundamental" to the *Prometheus*-theme does not stand up to chronological examination, and cannot be used to justify an earlier dating of the Contredanse.

33

Moreover, the argument ignores the differences in scoring between the ballet and the contredanse. The ballet is scored for a full complement of strings, winds and tympani; the contredanse uses just clarinet, horns, first and second violin, and violoncello/bass on a single line. When Deiters compares just the first four measures of the last with the opening measures of the bass line in the ballet, and draws his conclusion, he ignores the fact that the first four measures of the bass line of the contredanse correspond to the viola part in the ballet finale:

Fig. 11: Comparison of Bass line of Contredanse No. 7 (WoO 14) with Viola line of *Prometheus* finale

This is just how Beethoven would reduce a full orchestra score for use in a smaller-scale piece. The bass line of the contredanse is actually a *composite* of the first four measures of the viola line and the second four measures of the bass line in the score of the ballet finale:

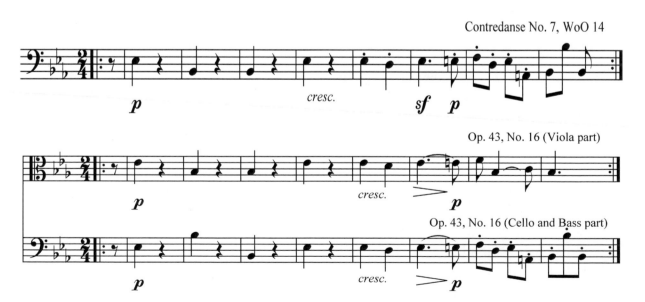

Fig. 12: Bass line of the contredanse is a composite reduction of the viola and bass lines of the ballet finale

This observation provides the missing linchpin for the counterargument to Deiters' assumption: there was a good and sufficient *reason* for Beethoven to "simplify" the bass line of the contredanse. He achieved the end result by combining the bass and viola parts into one melodic line. The fact that he had not yet, in November 1801, hit upon the idea of treating the bass line with its octave leap as a separate theme for its own variations, and going on from there to develop the whole *Prometheus*-melody into something extraordinary, explains why he was content to use the viola line, without the leap, for the first four measures of the contredanse.

As Shin Kojima has noted in his critical edition of the Contredanses, the evidence of the sketches, first editions and autographs is decisive on the point that the ballet came first, and it is high time to put to rest all argument and assumptions to the contrary.[95] I will summarize the evidence at this point, and deal with a few points raised by Fishman.

First, Gustav Nottebohm must be given his due. In 1865, in connection with his publication of a description of the Kessler sketchbook from 1801-1802, he called attention to the fact that sketches for the contredanses preceded those of the piano variations, and noted that the premiere of the ballet preceded the date of the first sketches in that book.[96] However, the Kessler sketchbook contains on its pages 9 and 10 sketches for just three of the twelve Contredanses that comprise WoO 14, namely, Contredanses nos. 2, 9 and 10. Nottebohm's observation, taken alone, does not definitively dispose of the question of the priority of the ballet over Contredanse No. 7. Sketches for two of the twelve Contredanses (Nos. 3 and 4), based on analysis of their watermarks, date from 1795.[97] Drafts of two more—Nos. 8 and 12—appear on the same folio as a piano trio which Beethoven published while he was still in Bonn, in 1791.[98] Thus it can readily be seen that the twelve were neither conceived of, nor composed, all at the same time. As the occasions presented themselves, Beethoven would write down ideas for dances, and when eventually he was commissioned to provide music for the ball season in the winter of 1801-1802, he gathered twelve of them into a set for publication.

The set of dances for which we have an autograph score was, accordingly, not viewed by Beethoven as an integral unit; nor was the particular order chosen seen as fixed.[99] The autograph, mostly in Beethoven's hand and dedicated by him to a "Monsieur de Friederich nomè Liederlich",[100] shows how the set was cobbled together: first comes a set of four, in what we are calling Contredanse No. 7 appears as the third among those first sketched in 1801-02, after the ballet's premiere: Nos. 10, 9, 7 and 2.[101] Then comes a pair (Nos. 5 and 1) written separately, with the notation over each "*par LvBthwn*"; from the watermarks, Kojima dates this part of the autograph also to 1801, but slightly earlier than the first part. Next come the two dances (Nos. 3 and 4) that date possibly from 1795, along with No. 6 (all on the same paper used for the 1795 sketches). Finally, on still a different kind of paper, which Kojima dates from 1799/1800, appear Nos. 8, 4 (again) and 12, written in the hand of Beethoven's brother Karl.[102] No. 11 is thus missing from the autograph altogether. The piano reduction, published by Mollo in 1802, contains only Nos. 8, 7, 4, 10, 9 and 1, in that order, although there exists a copyist's score for it which also has Nos. 2, 5 and 12, in this overall order: Nos. 1, 12, 10, 5, 4, 9, 7, 2, 8.[103]

The absences of No. 11 from the autograph score and from the piano version, and the duplication of No. 4 in the autograph, are thus most telling. One would think that if Beethoven had already written No. 11 before the ballet, a separate score of it would be handy to include in the autograph; the same would be true of the piano reduction. On the other hand, if the chronology were reversed, then it would have been very easy for Beethoven to include in the set orchestrated for the balls two dances from his recently composed, and reasonably successful, ballet.[104]

But do the sketches furnish more concrete evidence to support the conclusion that the most famous of the set, No. 7, was not composed earlier than the ballet itself? Nathan Fishman, in his commentary to the Wielhorsky sketchbook, thinks that they do.[105] He points out that Landsberg 7, the sketchbook which contains all of the known sketches for the ballet that premiered in March 1801, contains at least one sketch for the *Prometheus-* theme that is a precursor to the published version:

Fig. 13: Landsberg 7 Sketchbook, p. 139, lines 5-6 (transcribed by Mikulicz)

It will be noted that Beethoven sketched the theme as beginning with an interval of a sixth, instead of the third that begins the final version (Fig. 9, p. 29). One sees that this sketch relates to the ballet finale, rather than to the contredanse, both from its location on page 139 in the midst of other sketches for the ballet's last number, as well as from the trill-like figure in the second violin, which appears in the finale at measures 43-46, and not at all in the fully scored contredanse. Fishman reasons that if the contredanse were to have been composed first, and Beethoven had developed its melody in its finished form at that time, to be transferred intact to the ballet finale, there would be no explanation for why Beethoven would be trying out a rejected variant of the theme in sketching the ballet.

There is one slight problem with this argument. Far from being a "rejected" variant,

36

the version with the opening sixth *does* appear in the ballet finale, at measures 106-07 and 164-65:

Fig. 14: Excerpt from violin part for *Prometheus* finale

It would therefore be possible to argue that this example is theoretically consistent with the contredanse having been composed first, and that Beethoven was experimenting with the theme and taking it further in the ballet.

Other sketches for the ballet are similarly ambiguous: one notes, for example, that the octave leap after the fermata in the twelfth measure from the end of Fig. 13 is a variant that never made it into the published score—but it is not in the contredanse either. If one limits the search just to variants that were actually used in the finished work, one could cite additional evidence from the Landsberg 7 sketchbook that shows Beethoven experimenting with the *Prometheus*-theme in ways that are foreign to the contredanse. For example, on page 130, line 2, the following sketch fragment appears:

Fig. 15: Landsberg 7 Sketchbook, p. 130, line 2

Needless to say, the D-flat appearing in the second bar of the sketch is wholly foreign to the contredanse, while Beethoven uses it in measures 56, 120 and 170 of the ballet finale. The same is true of the following sketch for measures 51-54 of the finale (the earliest form of the *Prometheus*-melody which appears in the Landsberg 7 sketchbook; the next is Fig. 13):

Fig. 16: Landsberg 7 Sketchbook, p. 131, line 4—the earliest form of the *Prometheus*-melody in the sketches

Nevertheless, as noted with Fishman's own example earlier, none of these instances alone is definitive: they are as consistent with Beethoven having written the ballet before the contredanse as with his having written the contredanse first, and then experimenting with expanding the music for the ballet later. Fishman's argument is, in the end, inconclusive.

While each individual instance taken alone may be unconvincing, however, the totality of the evidence provided by the ballet sketches is far stronger. We must remember, first, that Beethoven also used in the finale music that he put into another of the twelve contredanses (No. 11, in G major). Mikulicz notes that the ballet sketches fill practically the entire second half of the Landsberg sketchbook, with the exception of shorter sketches for other works that are occasionally interspersed. There are sketches for all of the ballet's numbers, except for the eight-bar, introductory *Andante* that is No. 11. The sketches for the finale are found on pages 130-31, 138-39, 143, 151 and 157. Portions of the *Prometheus*-melody are sketched on line 2 of page 130 (Fig. 15 above), on line 4 of page 131 (Fig. 16 above), and on lines 5-6 of page 139 (Fig. 13 above). The only sketch we have for the section of the finale that uses Contredanse No. 11 music is this, on page 143, lines 3-4 (in the original, the notes are small because Beethoven wrote this passage in "Spitz", the small, pointed style he used for rapid sketching):

Fig. 17: Landsberg 7 Sketchbook, p. 143, lines 3-4 (transcribed by Mikulicz)

And here is the finished version from the ballet, with the violin line exactly as it also appears in Contredanse No. 11:

Fig. 18: Violin line of *Prometheus* finale and Contredanse No. 11 (WoO 14)

This is an example of Beethoven's habit of continually reshaping the thematic line, which he first conceives in its general proportions and harmony, until it is musically far superior to what he began with.[106] This time we *are* dealing with a rejected variant that was preliminary to both works, and Fishman's logic fully applies. The version in the sketch for the ballet is never used in the ballet, and instead the finished version of the ballet is the same as the published version of the contredanse. In combination with the evidence from the autograph and the piano version, therefore, one can only conclude that Contredanse No. 11 had not already been written by the time that Beethoven was working on the finale of *Prometheus*. This evidence, therefore, provides us with a clear example of Beethoven's adapting music he had conceived and written for the ballet as a dance to be used for the ball season of 1801-1802.

Now consider the relative placement of the sketches. Notice that they appear in the same order in the sketchbook that they do in the ballet finale. While arguments from the order of Beethoven sketches are notoriously shaky, given his habits of composition,[107] the order in this case is not a crux, but just one in a series of factors that require more and more conjectures to sustain the theory that the contredanse preceded the ballet. We are required, first, to conjecture that Beethoven conceived and wrote Contredanse No. 7 before March 1801 for no particular occasion that we know of, and that he put it on the shelf, so to speak, as we know he did earlier with Contredanses Nos. 8, 12, 3, 4 and 6. Then we are required to conjecture that when it came time to write the ballet finale Beethoven happened to remember Contredanse No. 7, out of all his other unpublished compositions (and in preference to the other four contredanses), and to select it for the lead rondo theme. This theory forces us also to explain the Landsberg 7 sketches as Beethoven's making successive creative experiments in elaborating the theme, most of which worked themselves into the finished ballet, but none of which gave Beethoven any cause to change the contredanse when he created its autograph some nine to ten months later. Finally, we must assume that when he received the commission for the ball dances,

39

and began to put the collection together, Beethoven found himself one short, and so reached back to a minor episode in the ballet finale to pluck a suitable candidate for Contredanse No. 11.

The conjectures the other way around are fewer and much more probable. We know (based on watermark evidence) that Beethoven already had composed Nos. 8, 12, 3, 4 and 6 before 1801. We are required to conjecture only that Beethoven composed the *Prometheus* ballet, during which he conceived the melodies used in the finale and elaborated them, and that after the ballet had received 14 performances he decided to use those same melodies in creating contredanses for a greatly diminished ensemble. In making the reduction of No. 7, the viola line was used in preference to that of the bass for the opening four measures. And that is all. Following Occam's principle, we are bound to prefer the simpler explanation.

As mentioned earlier, however, Beethoven himself supplies the most significant clue in this controversy, in the letter he wrote to his publisher Hoffmeister concerning the piano variations, op. 35:

"In the grand variations you have forgotten to mention that the theme has been taken from an allegorical ballet for which I composed the music, namely, *Prometheus*, or in Italian, *Prometeo*. This should have been stated on the title page. And I beg you to do this if it is still possible, that is to say, if the work has not yet appeared. If the title page has to be altered, well, let it be done at my expense."[108]

(Hoffmeister did not follow Beethoven's wish, which is why we are saddled with the anachronistic title "*Eroica* variations" for op. 35.) As Fishman asks: why should Beethoven, who was such a stickler for accuracy, go to such pains to have the ballet identified as the source of the theme for the variations if in fact it was a different work?[109] One cannot reply that the reason was that the ballet would be more familiar to the public—the dance had been performed throughout the ball season of 1801-02, and the piano reduction published and sold later in 1802, along with the piano reduction of the ballet music. Once again, the point is telling, but not conclusive on its own. The theory that the contredanse preceded the ballet has gained an academic momentum that is difficult to account for on the grounds of its explanation of the facts that we have.[110] The theory that the ballet came first explains matters much more satisfactorily.

Academic preference for the contredanse as first has tended to minimize the real significance of the *Prometheus*-theme in Beethoven's development as a composer. It has also needlessly complicated the analyses of the *Eroica*, by relegating the *Prometheus*-music to a secondary way station instead of according it its rightful status as the *Eroica*'s fount and origin.   As a corollary, there has been more room for theories that Napoleon (or other contemporary heroes, such as General Abercrombie or Lord Nelson) inspired the Symphony's genesis.   At the same time, it requires scholars to invent a reason why Beethoven would single out *this* particular contredanse for such special treatment in three subsequent works.[111]   In the process, the simplified and more realistic view provided by the hypothesis that the ballet was first has been lost.[112]

If much has been made of the controversy over which composition came first, it is because the outcome is of more than academic interest. Whether it is a fair judgment that the *Prometheus*-melody was of far more than ordinary significance to Beethoven, both musically and spiritually, depends on how one resolves the issue. One could conceivably propose that the identification of the melody with the myth of Prometheus became fixed in Beethoven's mind after his work on the ballet, regardless of whether that work came first or second. To argue from that standpoint, however, is to minimize the role that inspiration in the course of struggling with a particular work plays in the conceiving of a particular theme. The point is *precisely* that it makes a world of difference for our understanding of what Beethoven went through whether he conceived the theme in question as just another pretty tune (albeit one to which people could dance on equal terms, *pace* Thomas Sipe [*see* n. 111]), or instead as a melody in which culminated the striving for perfection of the two allegorical creatures in the ballet. It is not a question of chance—whether or not the theme just happened to fit the requirements—but a question of the compositional process, of design and intent. What matters is that Beethoven *went on* from that point to see that more, much more, could be done with the theme than he had accomplished with it heretofore, and that, once he came to that realization, he achieved by means of it a new synthesis of musical elements, a synthesis so radically different from what had gone before that generations of scholars are united in calling it the inauguration of Beethoven's *heroic* style.[113] In order to appreciate the process through which this development occurred, so important for all music that came afterwards, we now have to take up the composition of two of the works which helped to inaugurate it — the variations for piano Op. 34 and Op. 35.

Chapter 5:
The Piano Variations, Op. 34 and Op. 35

Drafts for Op. 34 and Op. 35 appear in both the Kessler and the Wielhorsky sketchbooks, as noted earlier. Beethoven completed his sketching of the variations, and presumably began work on autograph scores, toward the end of his stay at Heiligenstadt in 1802. In describing them on October 18 of that year to his publishers Breitkopf & Härtel, he says that both cycles are written in an entirely "new manner", and that the theme of each is "treated differently" from the other.[114] The meaning of these remarks in relation to Op. 34 undoubtedly has to do with the fact that each variation is in a different key (descending by thirds) and meter; a more detailed analysis of the entire cycle, fascinating though it is, would take us too far astray. Here the concern is with the cycles only as they are related to the *Eroica* Symphony. Thus Op. 35 will be dealt with *in toto*, but of Op. 34 only the fifth variation—the *Marcia* (*Allegretto*, 2/4, in C minor)—will be considered, because it alone is directly related to the subsequent composition of Op. 55.

If we compare this fifth variation with the theme of Op. 34, the nature of this relationship will become more apparent. The harmonic plan of the theme (in F major) is followed fairly closely, if we allow for the change from major to minor mode, and its melodic outlines are also retained in a number of places, but its character has been completely transformed. The title, *Marcia—Allegretto*, seems hardly sufficient to describe the new mood. And in fact, if one turns to the sketches, he will find that Beethoven has written above the first draft of this variation the title "*Todtenmarsch*", or "*Funeral March*":

Fig. 19: Wielhorsky sketches for op. 34, on page [Russ. "Stranitsa"] 16, lines I-III (hereinafter: "16/I-III")

The change in mood and character is so complete that Beethoven has written a special six-bar transition at the end of the variation in order to prepare for the return of F major in the sixth and concluding variation.

The striking similarity between the opening bars of this fifth variation and those of the second movement of the *Eroica* Symphony has been pointed out before, but in his edition of the Wielhorsky sketchbook, Fishman remarks that the similarity is nowhere so apparent as in the following early sketch (W16/XIII-XIV, and bars 1-4 of the Symphony's second movement—from now on, written as "55/2, 1-4"):[115]

Wielhorsky sketchbook, 16/XIII-XIV

Fig. 20: Wielhorsky sketch for op. 34 compared to published version of op. 55/2

The sketches demonstrate that the fifth variation of op. 34 is the next link in the chain which begins with Prometheus' death-music in the ninth number of the ballet, continues through the funeral march of the piano sonata Op. 26 to op. 34, and ends with the *Marcia funebre* of the Third Symphony. At no other time in his life was Beethoven so preoccupied with writing music for the death of a great hero than in these two and one-half years between the composition of *Die Geschöpfe des Prometheus* and the *Eroica* Symphony. It seems that the influence of the ballet music on subsequent works was not confined to the repeated use of a theme from its final number; concomitant to the legend of the hero's rebirth is the hero's death which must precede that rebirth. While this is not to suggest a programmatic content for all of Beethoven's works with funeral marches in them, it does help to explain the proportionately large number of such pieces in his works of this period, compared to earlier and later periods—works in which the influence of the *Prometheus* "life-music" is generally quite manifest.

The companion piece to Op. 34 is Op. 35, which was begun a little earlier than the former work. It is here, of course, that one finds evidence of the Promethean influence; the *Tema* for the Variations Op. 35 is the rondo melody of the ballet's finale, together with its bass. For the first time known to us, Beethoven in Op. 35 gives both melody and bass independent musical lives: each serves as a foundation for thematic development. The earliest sketches for op. 35, in the Kessler sketchbook, show that Beethoven realized the potential of developing the bass as a separate theme almost from the very first.[116] This feature by itself makes the Op. 35 cycle "variations [written] in a new manner", and also differentiates the cycle from Op. 34.

Op. 35 differs also in its unusual introduction—not only does Beethoven break out the bass as its own theme, but he *begins the entire work with it*:

Fig. 21: *Prometheus*-variations, op. 35 (Introduction)

Such a startling idea, which sets the stage for the full *Tema* only after the bass has been enveloped in counterpoint *A due*, *A tre* and *A quattro*, was entirely new for its time. As the reader is aware, Beethoven uses the same scheme in opening the finale of the *Eroica* Symphony. Fishman, followed by Maruyama and Cooper,[117] sees the explanation of this development as a summation (in highly condensed form) of the *Prometheus* scenario: the opening chord of Op. 35 depicts the life-giving touch of the heavenly fire (in Op. 55/4, the chords are preceded by the storm and raging of Zeus), and the *pianissimo* octaves of the bass are the creatures' subsequent first tentative steps. As they develop and progress to higher stages of awareness, the *Basso del Tema* moves to higher and higher registers and the counterpoint becomes successively more intricate. Finally the pinnacle of the process is reached as the theme itself is born from a previously established harmony.

45

It is a picturesque explanation, and perhaps not without some foundation. It is entirely possible that Beethoven liked the idea of developing the *Basso del Tema* separately at the beginning of the work because, when he played it (or heard it in his head), it called to mind his original music for the creatures; when the bass is stated *piano* (or *pizzicato,* as in the Symphony finale), it has the same character of tentativeness and incompleteness.[118] The listener knows at once that this is not all there is to come. But it is in this feeling of expectation, rather than in any intended synopsis of the ballet action, that Beethoven's procedure would seem to lie. By the time the *Eroica* Symphony was first performed publicly in 1805, no one had seen the *Prometheus* ballet for nearly three years, and as mentioned earlier, by the time the ballet music—other than the Overture—was first performed again in 1843, the ballet scenario had become lost (if it ever existed in the first place).[119] Thus it would have been a rare member of the public who could have appreciated Beethoven's intent to summarize in his introductory music the action of the ballet. (Indeed, the critic who wrote the long analysis of the *Eroica* for the *Allgemeine musikalische Zeitung*—one who might be expected to grasp any such intent on Beethoven's part—instead took Beethoven's music literally.[120] He analyzed the *bass theme* as the principal motif of the finale, and treated the *Prometheus*-melody itself as just counterpoint!) On balance, therefore, it seems best to say that the Introduction is precisely what its name implies—it prepares what is to follow. Beethoven hit upon the inspired idea of using the bass alone for this purpose, and the result is a new facet added to the familiar variation form.

The details of how he came to use the bass as a theme in its own right are disclosed, as far as one may discern, in the Kessler sketchbook, and have already been described in an article by Christopher Reynolds which fully analyzes all the Kessler and Wielhorsky sketches for Op. 35.[121] Beethoven appears first to have entertained the idea of beginning the work with the bass line stated in half-notes, in 2/4 meter (he has crossed these measures out in the original, but he retained the idea in the final version):

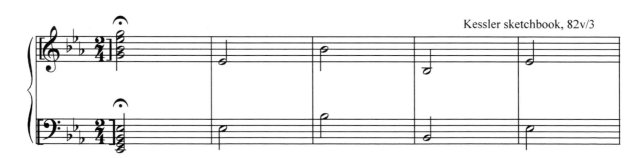

Fig. 22a: First sketch of *Basso del Tema* in the Kessler sketchbook

In his next sketches, he starts to experiment with how the bass (still stated in half notes) can be developed fugally:

Kessler sketchbook, 83r/V

Kessler sketchbook, 83r/XIV

Fig. 22b: Subsequent development of the *Basso del Tema* in Kessler

It was only later that he hit upon the "introductory" character of this theme when stated *piano* and *staccato*. But that is entirely typical of the process by which Beethoven would thoroughly develop and examine all the latent potentialities in any given theme. If the *piano* version was also partly occasioned by a memory of his music for the creatures' first movements in the ballet, who is to say that the coincidence was not a happy one?

The process of the working out of the subsequent variations and fugue of Op. 35 is well documented in the sketchbooks, and Christopher Reynolds has analyzed how Beethoven assembled the piece from its component parts (Reynolds 1982). None of that need be repeated here; instead, we will concentrate on the connections to be found between Beethoven's work on Op. 35 and his subsequent composition of the *Eroica*. This is not to treat Op. 35 as some sort of preliminary exercise for the composition of the Third Symphony; as Fishman notes in his commentary on the sketches: "No matter how glittering the shine of the *Eroica*, one cannot ignore that its closest satellite radiates not only a reflected light, but its own as well."[122]

The parallels between the published versions of the Third Symphony and Op. 35 have also been treated elsewhere.[123] While the Symphony finale follows fairly closely the Introduction of the Variations Op. 35 as far as the former's 108th bar, the development of the *Prometheus*-theme unfolds very differently in the Symphony after that, and any comparisons between the two works become forced.

The point instead is to note that Beethoven sketched and composed far more music for the variations than he eventually included in the published opus.[124] It is Fishman's contribution to show how the Symphony benefited from this fecundity, and he gives numerous examples of ideas that were conceived in the course of sketching the Variations but were not included in the published work, and which were instead conserved for use in the Symphony finale.[125] For example, among the sketches for the finale of the Variations is found the following draft on page 32 of Wielhorsky, at line V—it is for an accompaniment to the fugue theme which was not used in the published version, but which appears instead in bars 227-30 and 235-38 of the Symphony finale (reproduced on the second staff):[126]

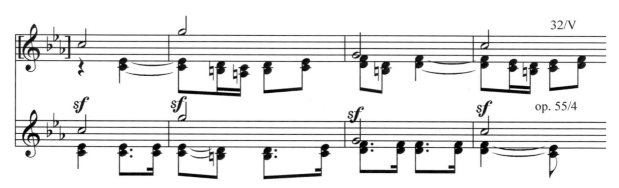

Fig. 23: Wielhorsky sketchbook (32/V) compared with *Eroica* finale, mm. 227-30; 235-38

Again, on page 27 of Wielhorsky is a draft for the middle section of the fifth variation of op. 35, a draft entirely different from Beethoven's final choice in that work. But Fishman compares it with the well-known oboe melody from the *Poco andante* of the *Eroica* finale (beginning at bar 365):[127]

Fig. 24: Wielhorsky sketchbook (27/IV) compared with *Poco andante* from op. 55/4

As a final example of the continuity that runs from the ballet to the Symphony,

Fishman cites a sketch from the last page of Landsberg No. 7 (*see* Fig. 25 below).[128] At the time Beethoven wrote it, Fishman believes he was considering using it in the tragic scene in No. 9. (Based on the material surrounding it, Mikulicz assigns it—somewhat incongruously, in my opinion—to the first number.) The idea surfaced again as Beethoven was working on the final sketches of the finale to Op. 35, and Beethoven once more rejected it in the finished score—only to resurrect it as what is now the well-known countersubject in the early bars (44-47) of the *Eroica*'s finale:

Fig. 25: Countersubject considered and rejected twice (1801 and 1802) by Beethoven before its incorporation into the *Eroica* finale, in 1803

Given that his initial sketches for a third symphony immediately follow this profligacy, one can only conclude that the sheer compositional abundance to which the *Prometheus*-theme inspired Beethoven must have, as part of the same process, given rise to the idea of embodying that same music in a work where it could receive fuller expression—-a symphony. And given the nature of the *Prometheus*-music itself, and what it signified to Beethoven (as discussed earlier), there can be no doubt that Beethoven's choice of that music as a subject for his symphonic work evinced his determination, after the crisis at Heiligenstadt, to show *virtue* in the face of undeserved adversity, and to let its triumph— as he had already experienced it in completing the op. 35 variations—be given full expression in a major new symphony.

Chapter 6:
From the Variations to the Symphony

As we have seen, Beethoven reached the end of the Kessler sketchbook without having completed his work on op. 34 and op. 35. Like the Kessler book, the Wielhorsky sketchbook had been already bound at Beethoven's request, and its 174 pages were ready to be filled.[129] The link between the two books is established in several ways. As Christopher Reynolds demonstrates, and as Sieghard Brandenburg independently discovered, there was a "back and forth" process between Kessler and Wielhorsky with regard to the sketches for op. 35, where Beethoven would sketch an idea in the opening pages of Wielhorsky, then transfer that idea back to a sketch he was still working on at the end of Kessler, and then finally take the idea as evolved there and transfer it back to Wielhorsky, where the sketch proceeded to completion.[130] With a few exceptions like these, all of the sketches for op. 34 and 35 in Wielhorsky are at a more advanced stage than those in Kessler. Another indicator is that the first two movements of the "Kreutzer" violin sonata, op. 47, are sketched toward the end of the Wielhorsky notebook, while the *Presto* finale of op. 47 is fully sketched in the Kessler notebook, along with sketches for the three violin sonatas of op. 30 — when Beethoven had plans to use the *Presto* movement as the finale for op. 30, No. 1.[131] The Kessler sketches show that he changed his mind and wrote a different finale for that work, and kept the *Presto* in reserve until, a year later, he conceived the Kreutzer sonata for a performance with the visiting violin virtuoso George Bridgetower in May 1803.

By its contents, Nottebohm dated the Kessler sketchbook as having been begun in October 1801, and continuing until approximately May 1802. The Wielhorsky sketchbook was thus begun also about May 1802; it finishes with the sketches for *Christus am Oelberge,* which received its premiere on April 5, 1803, and for the first two movements of the Kreutzer sonata. Many of its early pages contain finishing sketches for the piano variations op. 34 and 35. Beethoven's brother Karl, in a letter written to Beethoven's publisher Hoffmeister at the end of September 1802, referred to "six or seven variations for piano, but composed in a manner like nothing yet existing" ("6 oder 7ben Variationen für Klavier, aber auf Art gemacht wie noch keine Existiren").[132] When Hoffmeister (who wanted to deal with Beethoven directly)[133] did not reply, Karl offered *two* complete sets of variations to Hoffmeister's rivals, Breitkopf & Härtel, in a letter dated October 18, 1802.[134] From subsequent correspondence, it is clear that these are the variations subsequently published as op. 34 and op. 35.[135] The two dates on Beethoven's famous testament

51

written at Heiligenstadt are October 6 and 10, 1802 (Appendix H). From these facts it is easy to conclude that the Wielhorsky sketchbook accompanied Beethoven to Heiligenstadt, where Beethoven spent the summer of 1802 working chiefly on the piano variations. (Indeed, Fishman proposed that the sketchbook be called the "Heiligenstadt Sketchbook", but other scholars have not taken up the name.)

While he was at Heiligenstadt in that summer of 1802, there probably occurred that most famous of incidents, described by Beethoven's pupil Ferdinand Ries:

"Already in 1802 Beethoven suffered at various times from difficulty with his hearing, an evil that by itself would taper off again. He was so sensitive to the onset of his deafness that one had to be very careful not to make him aware of the defect by loud talk. If he did not understand something, he usually blamed it on absentmindedness, which to be sure was a trait he possessed to a high degree. He spent a great deal of the time in the country, where I often went to take a lesson from him. Frequently he would say after breakfast, at eight in the morning: 'Let us go first for a little walk.' So we would go for a walk, and often did not return until three or four o'clock, after having eaten something in some hamlet or another. On one of these outings, Beethoven gave me the first striking proof of the decline in his hearing, about which Stephan von Breuning had already spoken to me. I called his attention to a shepherd in the forest, who was playing rather well on a flute that had been fashioned out of lilac wood. Beethoven for a whole half hour could hear nothing at all, and grew extraordinarily still and scowling, even though I repeatedly assured him that I did not hear anything any longer either (which was, however, not the case) . . ."[136]

Although Ries's dating of this incident in 1802 may have been retroactively influenced by the publication of the Heiligenstadt Testament, in which Beethoven melancholically complains of a similar incident occurring during a walk in the woods, there should be no question that a combination of daily small reminders during the summer of 1802 brought home to Beethoven that his hearing loss would likely deteriorate until it became permanent, despite the best efforts of his Vienna doctors. This growing realization led both to the emotional outburst recorded in the Heiligenstadt Testament, and to the sheer energy he poured into his work on the piano variations, written "truly in an entirely new manner" and completed at the same time.

It is in this context that we assess the significant evidence presented on pages 44 and 45 of the Wielhorsky sketchbook, reproduced here in both facsimile and in Fishman's transcription. (*See* Plates 12-15 below.) It is late summer or early fall of 1802, and Beethoven has nearly finished his work on the piano variations op. 34 and 35, which have occupied almost all the first 43 pages of the document. Pages 34 through 43, in fact, are filled exclusively with sketches for the fugal finale of op. 35, in which the *Basso del Tema* is developed as a subject in its own right.

Plates 12-15: Pages 44-45 of Wielhorsky sketchbook in facsimile and Fishman's transcription

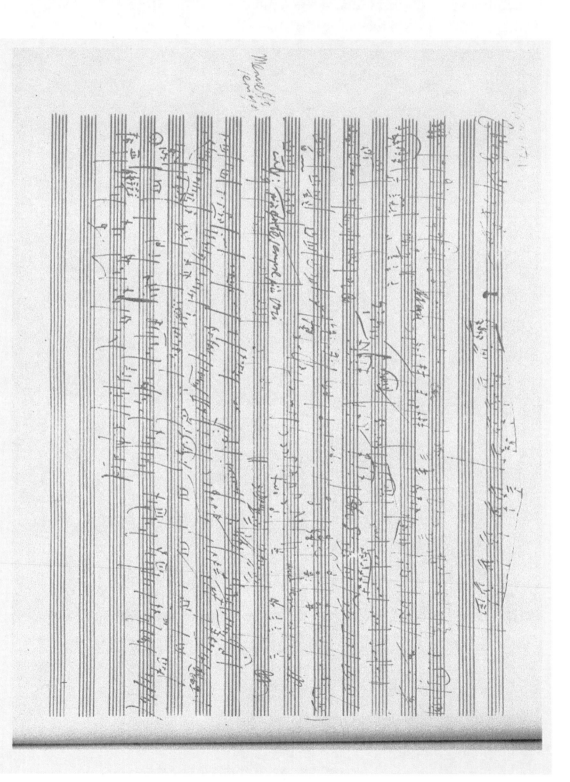

54

Страница 45

М. 27998 г.

On the first line of page 44 there is jotted down a fragment of the Bagatelle, op. 33, No. 1; after it come two bars of a piece not yet identified. A blank line follows, and then on the third line appears the outline of a broad melody in E-flat major, in 4/4 time, which transitions to a quicker theme in 3/4 time, also in E-flat. A few lines further down the words "*adagio C dur*" are written, and above the ninth line Beethoven has written "*Menuetto serioso*". The rest of page 44 and the whole of page 45 are taken up with music that is all in E-flat major and all in triple time.

If one looks closely at the left-hand margin of line III of the photographic facsimile of page 44 (p. 54), one can just make out, written faintly in pencil, the word "*Eroica*". How this word came to be written there, and what is the significance of the sketches on these two pages, is a story that Nathan Fishman was the first to tell in full.[137] I shall summarize here the salient points.

When Wilhelm von Lenz examined the sketchbook in Count Wielhorsky's library in the late 1850's, he made a number of brief notations in the margins of its pages. These were evidently to serve him as guides to the contents of the sketchbook when he prepared his description of it for his revised Catalog of Beethoven's Compositions published in 1860. His examination must have been a very hasty one, however, for among other errors, he wrote the word "Eroica" in several places in the sketches for op. 34 and op. 35 (*e.g.,* over the word "Todtenmarsch" which Beethoven wrote over the fifth variation of op. 34 on page 16). As Alexander Thayer shrewdly surmised, von Lenz had mistaken sketches for op. 35 to be sketches for the finale of op. 55.[138] In his published Catalog, von Lenz accordingly reported that the sketchbook contained "an indication of the *Marcia funebre* from the *Eroica* and continual sketches for the finale", which preceded sketches for the oratorio op. 85. He then compounded his error with those of Schindler and Ries mentioned earlier,[139] in which they had independently asserted that Beethoven was working on the sketches for *Christus am Oelberge* in the summer of 1800, and concluded that since sketches for the latter follow the "*Eroica*" sketches at some distance in Wielhorsky, Beethoven must have started work on the Third Symphony earlier in 1800, and must have continued at work on it for five years, until 1804.[140]

The meaning of the word "*Eroica*" on page 44 is thus unclear. The sketch on line III of this page is obviously not related either to the finale or to the *Marcia funebre* of op. 55. If von Lenz supposed that it was a sketch for a different movement, he did not report its existence in his Catalog. He must have been uncertain, but his caution did not protect him. When Ludwig Nohl visited St. Petersburg in 1871, he subjected the sketchbook to a thorough examination and of course discovered all of von Lenz's errors.

In his account of the sketchbook,[141] Nohl ridiculed von Lenz's identification of the sketches for op. 34 and op. 35 as sketches for op. 55, and singled out for particular obloquy the notation on page 44. He cites the first ten bars of the third line, "which is again marked '*Eroica*' by our man with the pencil!"[142] He goes on to observe that the piece sketched here cannot, by virtue of its character and the instrumental indications Beethoven has added, be a composition for the piano, "but is probably a symphony or quartet. The sketches for the Menuetto also fill page 45."[143]

Nohl has overlooked an indication of Beethoven's for a "*Fag.*" (bassoon) to play the melody written on the seventh line, and so the suggestion that the music might be for a quartet is unlikely. Moreover, in quoting the melody on line III, he misread for a double bar what is actually a treble clef sign, and erroneously transcribed two notes. Thus what he quotes as

Fig. 26: Wielhorsky sketchbook, tr. Nohl, p. 44, line III

is actually the following, which makes quite a difference in hearing what Beethoven intended:

Fig. 27: Wielhorsky sketchbook, tr. Fishman, p. 44, line III

Finally, Nohl assumed that Beethoven's notation "*Menuetto serioso*" applied not only to line IX of page 44, but to the rest of the lines on that page and to all of page 45 as well. As is evident from an examination of Fishman's transcription, however, the music on the tenth line is a revision of that found at the end of line III and the beginning of line IV, and has nothing to do with the sketch for the *Menuetto*, the sketch for which ends on the same line as it begins (line IX). (*See* Fishman's transcription, Plate 14.)

This fact has considerable significance, for if we return to line III, we find that the broad melody in 4/4 time which Nohl misquoted is in reality an *introduction* to a movement in 3/4 time which begins in the last measure of that line. The sketches for this movement are then interrupted by those for the *Adagio in C dur* and the *Menuetto serioso*, but are taken up again in a second draft of the movement which fills out the rest of page 44 and all of page 45. The main theme of this movement is quite obviously related to the *Basso del Tema* of the *Prometheus*-melody, which, one may recall, had just been occupying Beethoven's mind on the pages of the sketchbook immediately preceding these:

Fig. 28: Wielhorsky sketchbook, tr. Fishman, p. 44, line X

As Fishman initially concluded, and Lewis Lockwood following him has confirmed, pages 44 and 45 of the Wielhorsky sketchbook represent Beethoven's initial plan for a four-movement symphony in the key of E-flat major, in which the three movements sketched here were to culminate in a finale based on the work Beethoven had already done with the *Prometheus* theme.[144]

The Wielhorsky sketchbook thus supplies the missing link between the *Prometheus* music and the Third Symphony. It enables us to see in its entirety the organic process by which the latter evolved from the former. To be sure, we are still missing evidence for some of the interim stages: the opening sketches for the first movement in the *Eroica* sketchbook (Landsberg No. 6) are well advanced from those on pages 44 and 45 of Wielhorsky, and it is probable that Beethoven made some sketches in the winter of 1802-1803 which are now lost.[145] If, however, with the evidence supplied by the Kessler, Wielhorsky and *Eroica* sketchbooks, we now have the correct chronology of Beethoven's occupation with the idea of Prometheus, we may conclude that the sequence was as follows:

In early 1801 Beethoven, while working on the commission for *Gli uomini di Prometeo*, became inspired by the ideal of Prometheus as a Titan who brought enlightenment and deliverance to humans, but who in consequence suffered unjustly at the hand of the gods. Yet Prometheus endured his punishment nobly, and survived to elevate the humans to whom he had given life to the point where they were fit to consort with the gods themselves. In the course of composing the music for the ballet, he wrote both tragic music for the staged death of the hero, as well as a theme that expressed the joyful exuberance of the humans and Prometheus in their concluding triumph.

In summer 1801 Beethoven wrote the first lengthy descriptions we have of his increasing deafness to his old friends Franz Wegeler and Carl Amenda,[146] in which he confides that "Often have I cursed the creator and my existence, [but] Plutarch has taught me resignation; I will, if it's otherwise possible, brave my destiny, even though there will be moments in my life when I will be the most miserable of god's creatures."[147]

In November 1801 Beethoven assembled an autograph score of a dozen contredanses,

60

some of which were commissioned by a "Monsieur de Friederich" for the forthcoming ball season in Vienna. Included in the set, as the third of the first group of four, was a version of the theme he used in the finale of *Prometheus,* which by then had enjoyed some thirteen performances at the Hoftheater and was a moderate success. Added at the last minute was another dance taken from the same finale. In the same month, Beethoven confided to his friend Wegeler that although his deafness continued to get worse, and that he was not satisfied with results from the treatments prescribed by his doctors, he was nevertheless enjoying again "einige seelige Augenblicke" ("a few blessed moments"), because he was in love with a young woman ("*Mädchen*") who loved him, and whom he hoped, despite their difference in rank, he could marry.[148] This was most likely the sixteen-year-old Countess Giulietta Guicciardi, then one of his piano students, who may have played the coquette with Beethoven, but who never seems to have seriously entertained the idea of marrying him.[149] Alexander Thayer speculated that Beethoven might have converted the dance from the *Prometheus* finale "so that it would become better known",[150] but this ignores the fact that there were *two* dances so adapted, as well as the fact of the popularity which the ballet already enjoyed. Speculation in a similar vein might entertain the thought that Beethoven wanted to impress with his compositions the young Countess, who doubtlessly partook of the ball scene in 1801-02, and that (subconsciously?) he reached back to a theme that already embodied his ideal that low-born humans could attain, through proper instruction in the arts, the ability to dance on equal terms with the gods (*sc.* the Viennese nobility) themselves.

The first part of 1802 was taken up by Beethoven's struggles to get his music published at what he considered a fair price, and increasingly he left negotiations to his brother Karl. He concentrated on finishing the violin sonatas op. 30 and the piano sonatas op. 31. His loss of hearing continued despite a variety of treatments, and on his doctor's recommendation he retreated in April to the quiet countryside of Heiligenstadt for some rest.

In the summer of 1802, at Heiligenstadt, the enormity of the loss he was enduring was brought home to him one day by the incident with the shepherd playing his flute. It is at this point that Beethoven seems to have seen himself as a modern-day Prometheus, unjustly tormented by fate, who returns to the music he has written for the ballet and determines to write a massive set of piano variations based on it. In the course of sketching the variations, he tries out the bass of the theme as a fugue subject, and a whole new world of inspiration opens up.

In October 1802, still at Heiligenstadt, Beethoven commits all his despair and self-doubt to paper, in a "testament" for his brothers intended to be read after his death (*see*

Appendix H). Within a few weeks of that low point, when he declared that he was kept from suicide only by his art, Beethoven completes his work on the fugal finale of the *Prometheus* variations op. 35. His ideas for the theme are far from exhausted: he turns to a fresh page, and lays out a plan for the first three movements of a new symphony, whose first movement is thematically linked to the *Basso del Tema*, and whose fourth movement will build upon the work he has already done with the theme.

Nota bene: Page 44 of the Wielhorsky sketchbook shows us the moment of conception of the *Eroica*. There is nothing in the sketch or the surviving documents from Heiligenstadt to support any theory of its origin other than that it grew out of the wealth of ideas Beethoven had generated in sketching the *Prometheus* variations. In particular, there is nothing in this evidence to suggest that the Symphony was conceived as a means of honoring Napoleon Bonaparte (or any other contemporary hero). The first hint that Beethoven was entertaining such an idea comes one year later, after Beethoven had *finished* sketching the work, in a letter written by his pupil Ferdinand Ries.[151]

Later in 1802, after returning to Vienna, Beethoven became embroiled in a lengthy and bitter controversy over the publication rights to his string quintet, op. 29, at the same time he was seeing to the details of publication for the variations op. 34 and 35.[152] In early 1803 he was engaged by the Theater an der Wien to compose an opera. He received also living quarters there and the right to give a concert of his works. He had a new symphony (the Second) and a piano concerto (the Third) to perform, but wanted to present a choral work as well. Still obsessed with the concept of a beleaguered hero, he was drawn to the libretto prepared by Franz Huber for *Christus am Oelberge* (*Christ on the Mount of Olives*), depicting Jesus's last hours before his capture by soldiers. After collaborating with Huber on the text, he worked intensively on the music of the oratorio until its first performance, on April 5, 1803. As Barry Cooper has postulated, passages expressing Jesus' anguish and terror at his impending suffering resonated with Beethoven's own innermost feelings as expressed in the Heiligenstadt Testament.[153] There was no need to turn back to his *Prometheus*-ideas while the oratorio was on his mind.

In May 1803, after performing his "Kreutzer" sonata with George Bridgetower, Beethoven rented rooms for the summer in a house in Oberdöbling, outside of Vienna. Here, as can be seen in the *Eroica* sketchbook, he works mostly on the first three movements of his new symphony, and surpasses in scope anything he has written before. The first-movement theme from Wielhorsky is now replaced by a continuous melodic line that is still thematically linked to the theme of the finale;[154] there are probably missing sketches that document this transition. In four large sketches he develops the plan of the movement until it exceeds in length any entire symphony theretofore written.[155] From the outset he had planned a slow march in C major / C minor for the second movement; reaching back to his ideas beginning with the Prometheus death-music from the ballet, he now transforms them into a stately *Marcia funebre* that attains extremes of expression never before put into music. With this movement mostly finished, he turns to the third, and the *Menuetto serioso* is quickly transformed into a lively scherzo, punctuated by a trio of horns.[156] The opening of the fourth movement contains strong parallels both to Act I of the ballet and to the introduction of op. 35, and work on it proceeds rapidly as the summer draws to a close.

In the fall of 1803, back in Vienna, Beethoven puts finishing touches on the fourth movement, which he performs at the piano for his boyhood friend Stephan Breuning and a guest.[157] His genius has now transformed the *Prometheus*-music into far more than just a fugue with variations. As others have noted, the *Eroica* finale is an apotheosis of musical form that in its inimitable way reprises both the opening scene of Act I as well as the varied divertissements enacted for Apollo on Parnassus in Act II of the ballet.[158] As such, it encapsulates Beethoven's entire experience with, and transformation achieved through, the Prometheus ideal.

In October 1803 we have the first indication of Beethoven's intention to dedicate the Symphony to Napoleon,[159] probably in connection with his plans to leave Vienna and move to Paris.[160] He grows more cautious in December, when Ries writes that he will not sell the Symphony, but take it with him to Paris.[161] His plans do not take into account the gathering clouds of war.

In the spring of 1804 we find that Beethoven has sold the Symphony after all, to his patron Prince Lobkowitz, and that the unusual arrangement includes the provision of both a rehearsal room (now called the *Eroica*-Saal in the Palais Lobkowitz in Vienna) and a full orchestra, with the requisite three horns, to try out the work before its public performance.[162] As a result, we can fix the date of the *Eroica*'s completion in score as early June 1804.

May 1804, on the other hand, is the usual date given for the famous incident described by Ferdinand Ries,[163] when Beethoven reacted with anger to the news that Napoleon had accepted his proclamation as Emperor of France, by ripping the title-sheet of the Symphony score in two and throwing it to the floor. However, this date is difficult to reconcile with subsequent letters of Beethoven: in July 1804 he wrote to Gottlob Wiedebein, a church organist, and mentioned he was still planning to leave Vienna the coming winter, probably for Paris;[164] and in August 1804, he wrote Breitkopf & Härtel offering them the Symphony to publish in score, and said it was "eigentlich betitelt [B]onaparte" ("actually entitled 'Bonaparte'").[165] The resolution of these paradoxes may lie

63

in recognizing what actually went on in France at this time. The French senate passed a resolution offering Bonaparte the imperial title on May 18, 1804, and Napoleon gave his assent that same day. However, the acts of the senate awaited ratification by a plebiscite, which did not occur until November 6, and Napoleon was not publicly *crowned* emperor of the French until the ceremony in Nôtre-Dame Cathedral on December 2, 1804. While Beethoven was an avid reader of newspapers, he may simply have missed the May announcement, or else may have counted on the plebiscite to stave off the end of the French republic. Ries's description makes it sound as though Beethoven was reacting to the news of the December coronation, in which Napoleon showed his true bent by seizing the imperial crown from the Pope and placing it on his head himself.

In August 1804 Beethoven has a working score entitled *"Sinfonia grande / [intitolata Bonaparte] / del Sigr / Louis van Beethoven* (*see* Plate 16, next page).[166] At a later date, the words *"intitolata Bonaparte"* ("entitled 'Bonaparte'") have been scratched out so severely that there are three holes in the title sheet at that point. In a darker ink, and a different hand, is written "804 im August" right under the scratched-out dedication. Under the name of the composer (note that it is given in French), Beethoven has scrawled in pencil (now greatly faded and hard to read), *"geschrieben auf Bonaparte"* ("composed on Bonaparte"). Thus the scratching out of the words *"intitolata Bonaparte"* may have occurred the following December, when the republican Beethoven finally realized that he could not go to Paris to live as the subject of one who had destroyed the French republic by crowning himself emperor. Even then, he could not disavow entirely his intention to connect the Symphony with Napoleon, and added his note in pencil. At the bottom of the title page are the words *"Sinfonia 3"* and at the right, *"op. 55"*. These obviously were added to the title page much later, when the Symphony could be assigned an opus number.[167] Note, however, that even then the Symphony has not received its final title of *"Eroica"* —that word is missing completely from the title page.

In December 1804 Beethoven conducted a performance of the *Eroica* in Prince Lobkowitz' palace, followed by another performance the next month at the home of the banker Joseph Würth. The first public performance of the Symphony took place in the Theater an der Wien on Palm Sunday, April 7, 1805, where its reception was decidedly mixed.[168]

In June 1805 Breitkopf & Härtel returned the score of the Symphony to Beethoven,[169] who had demanded its return when they indicated they were not willing to pay the price he asked for it.[170] The orchestral parts were not published until October 1806, when—for the first time— Beethoven called the work *"Sinfonia Eroica"*, and added the words *"composta / per festiggiare il sovvenire di un grand Uomo"*. The work was dedicated, not to Napoleon, but to Beethoven's loyal patron, Prince Lobkowitz (Plate 1, p. ix).

Plate 16: Title Page of *Eroica* Autograph Score

Chapter 7:
Summary and Conclusion

Beethoven and the idea/mythos of Prometheus. For Beethoven, Prometheus was an idealized mythical figure with whose adversities he could identify: as he became painfully aware of his impending deafness, he could draw strength from the story of the Titan who stoically endured an unjust punishment for having brought gifts to mankind (life-giving fire, and in Viganò's scenario, music and all the arts as well). But he did not "heroicize" Prometheus—who was already a Titan, after all. If one analyzes the ballet, there is nothing beyond the opening music that was given as a solo to the dancer in the role of Prometheus. Instead, it is Prometheus *together with* the star dancers—Signora Casentini, in the role of the woman, and Viganò himself, as the man—who dance at the culmination of the work, where the "*Prometheus*-melody" repeatedly makes its appearance.

There is thus nothing in the finale music, or in the choreography one would expect from Viganò, to allow one to conclude that this melody was exclusively identified with just Prometheus. Rather, in a finale where both gods and humankind are celebrating, the music represents the summit of human achievement—whereby man and woman have earned, through their avid development with the help of Prometheus and the other gods, the right to consort with them, to jubilate with them, and—let it be said—to greet them as equals (other than for the slight problem of mortality). But the pains of mortality are forgotten in the jubilant music of the finale. Melpomene's dance is left far behind, without an echo to suggest its continued presence.

It is just in this context that one has to appreciate the significance of the "*Prometheus*-melody" for Beethoven: it encapsulated for him the progress mankind could make with the help of the arts, particularly when he found that its bass could be treated separately, then built up *A due*, *A tre* and *A quattro*, and so provide a miniature of the humans' tentative steps on the way to mastery. In short, by calling it a "*Prometheus*-melody", we must take the name Prometheus to refer not to the god himself, but to the story of the whole ballet, which resonated fully with Beethoven's philosophy.

This is not to downplay the significance of the Prometheus myth for Beethoven personally. Given that he wrote the Heiligenstadt Testament while he was finishing the op. 35 piano variations, the importance of his identification with an unjustly punished gift-giver in helping him through his crisis of confidence cannot be understated. But by the time that Beethoven had completed opus 35, and began immediately to work on the plan for an E-Flat Major symphony in which this melody would play a culminating role, the music itself had come to mean much more for Beethoven than just an expression of his relationship to, or identification with, the myth. It symbolized for him the full import and purpose of his mission as composer—to express in glorious sound the degree to which man could aspire to Olympian heights through music—*his* music, Beethoven's music. And since only he could bring this work to full fruition, the music itself became the golden thread that pulled him through his labyrinth of despair ("Hope creat[ing] / From its own wreck the thing it contemplates"[171]). It brought him to new powers of expression, and strengthened his confidence in wielding them—witness the wholly unprecedented form, and the unbounded energy, of the *Eroica* finale, to say nothing of the *Eroica* as a whole. The glory of Beethoven's *Prometheus*-music is that, through its use at four different times in this crucial stage of his career, it allows us literally to hear, as in no other sequence of works, and by the use of a single theme, the breakthrough which Beethoven made from the classical to the romantic world.

The Eroica and Napoleon. Having set this context for the *Eroica,* we now ask: Where does Napoleon fit in? There have been many attempts to synthesize Napoleon with Prometheus; the scholarly urge to do so is irresistible, and is given impetus by the connection, through Viganò, with Vincenzo Monti's epic poem *Il Prometeo,* dedicated by its author to Bonaparte. I shall not add to them.

To me, the case needs no such connection, or synthesis: it is abundantly clear that, having just finished a major new work, and thinking he wanted to move permanently to France, Beethoven was trying to use the only economic power that he had to bring about such a move, by dangling the prospect that he would dedicate it to a person of such importance.[172] It also must have been intellectually satisfying to Beethoven to regard Napoleon (for a time, at least) as a present-day embodiment of the Promethean ideal. Perhaps it was in this sense that he wrote "geschrieben auf Bonaparte" ("composed on Bonaparte") across the title page of the *Eroica.* (He could just as accurately have written "geschrieben auf Prometheus", but only he would have understood the reference, while everyone could relate to Napoleon. And, so long as one is angling for maximum economic benefit from a new score, it does not hurt to flatter the powerful dedicatee even more—what does it matter if there is that funeral march to explain?)

It is also clear that when Napoleon thwarted Beethoven's hopes of a move to Paris, by literally crowning himself Emperor, Beethoven reacted in the only way his republican soul allowed: first in anger, by scratching out the dedication (actually, more than a dedication—an "entitling" ["*intitolata*"]), and then in irony and satire, by inscribing on the title page that the symphony was "composed to honor the *memory* of a great man". (Emphasis supplied by the present author; the irony is Beethoven's.)

There yet remained indelible the stamp of Prometheus on the Symphony; no mortal's failings could rob it of its integrity. Such an observation suggests why, perhaps, despite his falling out with Napoleon, the Symphony remained Beethoven's favorite for the rest of his life.[173] At a time of increasing despair and anguish over his impending deafness, Beethoven rallied his creative forces around the figure of a Titan who refused to surrender to an unjustly imposed punishment. His work on the ballet *Prometheus*, and the theme which arose from that work, became the vehicles by which the composer brought himself to a new threshold of creativity, which was to be of deepest significance musically for himself and for the nineteenth century.

APPENDICES

Appendix A: History of the "Wielhorsky" Sketchbook

Beethoven's sketchbook used during the years 1802 and 1803 was published for the first time in 1962 as *Kniga èskizov Betxovena za 1802-1803 gody*, 3 vols., edited by Nathan L. Fishman (Moscow: Gosudarstvennoj Muzykal'noj Izdatel'stvo [State Musical Press], 1962). The volumes are not numbered, and in this book "Vol. I" is the facsimile, "Vol. II" is the transcription, and "Vol. III" is the commentary; the work itself is cited as: "Fishman". It set the standard for future editions of the Beethoven sketchbooks, by making available both an editorial transcription and a photographic facsimile for ready comparison. Prior editions had consisted only of transcriptions (*e.g.*, Gustav Nottebohm, *Ein Skizzenbuch von Beethoven* [Leipzig: Breitkopf & Härtel, 1865] [the "Kessler" sketchbook, or "N 1865"], and *Ein Skizzenbuch von Beethoven aus dem Jahre 1803* [Leipzig: Breitkopf & Härtel, 1880] [the "*Eroica*" sketchbook (Landsberg 6), or "N 1880"]; Karl Mikulicz, *Ein Notierungsbuch von Beethoven* [Leipzig: Breitkopf & Härtel, 1927] [Landsberg 7]), or of facsimiles (*e.g.*, *Ludwig van Beethoven Skizzenbuch* [Leipzig: Verlag Wilhelm Engelmann, 1913]), but not both together. (The early sketchbook editions from the Beethovenhaus had provided a transcription in the form of a "printed facsimile", which tried to reproduce all of Beethoven's markings in print just as he had written them on the page.) *See generally* Johnson 1978 for a history of Beethoven sketch and sketchbook publications.

How the sketchbook got to Moscow after Beethoven's death is unknown. It was first described by Wilhelm von Lenz as part of his discussion of *Christus am Oelberge* (op. 85) in an updated catalog of Beethoven's works appended to the third volume of his *Beethoven: Eine Kunststudie* (Lenz 1855/1860), where he stated (pp. 221-23) that the sketchbook was in the library of Count Wielhorsky in St. Petersburg. Since von Lenz had published an earlier version of his catalog as part of his *Beethoven et ses trois stiles* (Lenz 1852) in which he did *not* refer to the sketchbook, and since von Lenz was a friend of the Count who had done research in the latter's library since the 1830's, Fishman surmises that Wielhorsky must have acquired the sketchbook sometime between 1852 and 1856, the year of the Count's death, or if it was acquired by his estate, then between 1856 and 1859. The book was subsequently inspected and described by Ludwig Nohl (Nohl 1874,

95-101).   Last mentioned as being in a private library in Moscow in 1900, the book dropped out of sight just before the Russian Revolution, and it was reported abroad as having been lost (Hess 1939).   It was in fact inventoried in a government archive in 1917, but its full significance was not appreciated until its existence came to the attention of the Moscow Conservatory of Music in 1939.   Fishman, vol. III, pp. 21-22.   For a fuller account of the sketchbook and its history, I set out in the following pages my translation (*see* Appendix to Haley 1966) of Fishman's text, Vol. III, pp. 13-22:

[Text of Haley (1966) translation of Fishman (1962), vol. III, at p. 13 begins here:]

The most important Beethoven manuscript now in the Soviet Union — both in respect to length and number of compositions represented — is the sketchbook which lies in the manuscript section of the M. I. Glinka Museum [in Moscow] under the catalog heading 155 No.1. This is the book with which the present publication is concerned. There are 174 pages (23 x 32 [centimeters]) in the book, each of which is lined in a sixteen-staff system. Beethoven's handwriting fills 168 of the pages (1-97, 102-105, 107-158 and 160-174). Six pages are blank.

The book is in comparatively good condition. All the pages are intact, and the ink has not faded. The single defect is that the upper part of one of the pages is torn off. This fact was known to Ludwig Nohl, who examined the sketchbook in the 1870's.[1]
An unknown person has numbered the odd pages in an accurate and fair hand, and has written the figure 19 on the remaining part of the defective page (the pagination was thus done after the page had been torn). On the cover and on the lower lines of the last page (174) another handwriting — but still not Beethoven's — has written the number 64, the meaning of which will become clear a little later.

In the quality and color of the paper, and also in the staff system, all the pages are identical. This characteristic, which would appear to be wholly an outward one, establishes an important difference between this document and others — which are analogous, but which contain pages of varied form and color — bound post factum, after the composer's work on the pieces in them had been completed. Separate pages and small notebooks were bound in this way according to their contents, and for this reason the chronological order of the various sketches in them was not always maintained. The sketchbook here published, however, is complete as an entity and was bound before

---

[1] L. Nohl, *Beethoven, Liszt, Wagner* (Vienna, 1874), p. 96.

Beethoven wrote his first sketches in it.

From this it by no means follows that the chronology of the sketch work corresponds exactly to the order of the pages. It is quite clear that, once having planned the beginning of some work (or section of a work), Beethoven would leave the next lines (or pages) empty and start the composition of something new further on in the book. Then, when he returned to continue what he had begun earlier, the number of lines which he had foreseen he would need was sometimes not enough for him, and in these cases there arose the peculiar "strip-farming" which coupled together sketches unrelated to one another.

And so, since the book's pages are in the same order today as they were when the composer wrote on them, it has not been impossible for the researcher to restore approximately the chronology of the sketches, by means of some change or another in the statement of a musical idea, and sometimes by means of a technical detail (the color of the ink, the change of a pen, the arrangement of the sketches on the lines, the bold or the restrained quality of the writing, and so on). In the transcribing of the complete book the element of chance was removed from this reconstruction by the fact that the pages comprise an entity.

The contents of the sketchbook consist of sketches for the following compositions:

1. Sonata in E-Flat Major for Piano, Op. 31, No.3
2. a. First movement
3. b. Second movement
4. c. Fourth movement
5. Variations in F major for Piano, Op. 34 (·Six Variations")
6. Variations in E-Flat Major for Plano, Op. 35 ("Fifteen Variations and Fugue")
7. Bagatelle in D Major, Op. 119, No. 3
8. Bagatelle in E-Flat Major, Op. 3, No. 1
9. Symphony No. 3 in E-Flat Major, Op. 55 ("Eroica")
10. a. First movement
11. b. Second movement
12. c. Third movement
13. Trio for Soprano, Tenor and Bass with Orchestra, "Tremate, empi, tremate," Op. 116 (text by Bettoni)

14. Duet for Soprano and Tenor with Orchestra, Nei giorni tuoi felici," without opus (to a text from the final scene of the first act of Metastasio's Olympiada)

15.   Oratorio *Christus am Ölberg*, Op. 85 (text by Huber)

16.   a. No.1. Recitative and Aria for Tenor

17.   b. No.2. Recitative and Aria for Soprano

18.   c. No.3. Recitative and Duet

19.   d. No.4. Recitative and Chorus

20.   e. No.5. Recitative and Chorus

21.   f. No.6. Recitative, Trio and Chorus

22.   g. Introduction

23.   Sonata in A major for Violin and Piano, Op. 47 ("Kreutzer")   a. First movement   b. Second movement

24.   Fragments of unknown works in piano version

25.   a. in G Major and C Major, of folk-dance character

26.   b. in E-Flat Major, in the character of a fast march

27.   c. in C Minor

28.   d. Two Fugues in C Major

29.   e. Rondo pour tous les instruments in F Major

30.   f. a series of other fragmentary sketches

31.   Unknown vocal works

32.   a. Adagio and canon in A Minor

33.   b. Canon in G Major

34.   Fragments of etudes, virtuoso piano formulas, cadences and exercises

The book is not dated by the author, but the period of time in which the work went on may be established by comparisons with other documents. An especially significant comparison is provided the book of sketches acquired in the auction after Beethoven's death by Karl Stein, and which afterwards belonged to the pianist Joseph Kessler. Since 1899 it has been kept in the library of the Gesellschaft der Musikfreunde in Vienna. This book, known to Beethoven scholars as the Kessler sketchbook, was described by Gustav Nottebohm, who established that Beethoven had been occupied with it between autumn of 1801 and spring of 1802.[2] It opens with sketches for a "Sacrificial Song" to words of F. Matthisson, and then follow further sketches related to:

three Contradances (from the twelve)

the Bagatelle, Op. 33, No. 6

the finale of the Second Symphony

the Trio, Op. 116

the first two movements of the Sonata in A Major, Op. 30, No.1

the finale (Presto) of the Sonata in A Major, Op. 47 ("Kreutzer")

the Sonata in C Minor, Op. 30, No.2

the Bagatelle, Op. 119, No. 5

the Sonata in D Minor, Op. 31, No.2

the Sonata in G Major, Op. 30, No. 3

the finale (*Allegretto con variazioni*) of the Sonata in A Major, Op. 10, No. 1

the Variations, Op. 35

the Variations, Op. 34

the Sonata in G Major, Op. 31, No.1

From the list cited it is evident that the Second Symphony and the Kreutzer Sonata are represented in the Kessler sketchbook by their last movements only. This might lead one to think that Beethoven was occupied earlier with the composition of their preceding movements, i. e., before autumn of 1801. And in fact, many sketches for the early movements of the Second Symphony are found in the sketchbook for 1800-1801 (the so-called Landsberg sketchbook).[3] But there is not a single note in it related to the first movements of Op. 41.

Why is the Kreutzer Sonata represented in the Kessler sketchbook only by the *Presto* finale? Why was the Presto written at the same time as the first movements of the Sonata Op. 30, No. 1? The explanation is simple. When he was composing the Presto, Beethoven intended it for the concluding movement of the Sonata Op. 30, No. 1 in A Major. Then, finding it unsuitable for that Sonata, he wrote a new finale for that work —

---

[2] *Cf.* G. Nottebohm, *Ein Skizzenbuch von Beethoven aus dem Jahre 1801*(Leipzig 1865).

[3] This is a book from the collection of L. Landsberg, and was published in Leipzig in 1927 by K. L. Mikulicz under the title *Ein Notierungsbuch von Ludwig van Beethoven.*

the Allegretto con variazioni. The *Presto* remained in reserve and took its place a year later in the new Sonata in A Major, the one dedicated to Kreutzer (Op. 47).

Since the sketches for the first two movements of Op. 47 appear in the sketchbook here published,[4] we may conclude that this sketchbook follows chronologically the Kessler sketchbook. Such a conclusion is fully supported when the sketches for the two sets of variations are compared with each other. In the Kessler sketchbook the Variations Op. 34 and 35 appear only in the last pages; moreover, of Op. 34 only the opening two bars of the theme and the first four bars of the sixth variation are sketched, and of Op. 35 only the inchoate version of the final Andante. But in the Beethoven sketchbook now in the Glinka Museum the same sets of variations, together with the Sonata Op. 31, No.3, occupy the first forty-three pages and virtually reach the form which they assumed in publication. The work of Beethoven's in question thus appears to be a direct continuation of that accomplished in the early spring of 1802.

Now it is necessary to look at two intermediate dates:

On October 18, 1802, Beethoven informed the publishers Breitkopf and Härtel that he had finished the work on the two sets of variations.[5] Thus by autumn of 1802 the first forty-three pages of the book were already filled.

On November 23, 1802, Beethoven's brother Karl wrote the publisher Johann Andre in Offenbach-am-Main: "Ludwig is not occupied with trifles at present, but is writing only operas and oratorios."[6] From this it may be concluded that at the beginning of winter the oratorio Op. 85 was not yet finished (the sketches for the oratorio begin to appear on page 90 of the sketchbook).

But on April 5, 1803 the oratorio was presented in a concert in the Theater-an-der-Wien. There must have been some time in between to allow for the final polishing of the work, the writing of the score, the copying and the learning of the solo parts, and the conducting of choral and orchestral rehearsals. Looking over the sketches up to the last page, one is easily convinced that they are still far from being ready to be put into score. The last page could not have been written later than several days before the

---

[4] *See* pages 166-173 of the sketchbook.

[5] A. Kalischer, *Beethovens sämtliche Briefe*, Bd I-V. Berlin, 1907-1908, letter No. 57.

[6] A. W. Thayer, *Ludwig van Beethovens Leben* (Leipzig, 1901-1911), Bd II, p. 358.

performance.

And so Beethoven worked on this sketchbook between April 1802 and March 1803.

Since he spent half of the year, from spring to late autumn of 1802, in Heiligenstadt — a village near Vienna — we shall hereinafter refer to the sketchbook — in distinction to the others — as the "Heiligenstadt sketchbook".

* * *

How did the Heiligenstadt sketchbook come into the Moscow museum, and who were its previous owners? Neither on the book's cover or on any of its pages are there any names, stamps or seals that might serve as indications to the book's previous whereabouts. Marks are found, however, on the margins of various pages — annotations, which point to a clue.

One of these marks is the word "Eroica",· written on the margins of pages 12, 16, 22, 28, 34, 37, 44, and others connected with the Sonata Op. 31, No.3, with the bagatelles and the oratorio. Evidently the author of the annotations examined the entire sketchbook. But he annotated some works several times, and paid no attention to others. He has not at all named the Variations Opp. 34 and 35, the duet to Metastasio's text, or the Terzett. The sketches for the "Kreutzer" are also left alone, but the designation "Op. 47" is conferred upon a fragment unrelated to the Sonata. The Bagatelle in D is marked not by its generally known opus number, 119, but by the number of the previous set — 112.

These peculiarities are described also in the "Catalog of Beethoven's Compositions, compiled by Wilhelm von Lenz and published in Hamburg in 1860.[7] Lenz talks about the "Skizzenbuch," where "by the sporadically legible words, since the sketches are illegible," rough drafts for the oratorio Op. 85 are recognized.[8] Of the sketches for instrumental works, Lenz mentions in passing the initial section of Op. 3, No.1, Op. 112, No.2, Op. 31, No. 3, one passage from the Sonata Op. 47, and an allusion to the "Marcia funebre" of the *Eroica* and sketches for its finale.[9]

Both in the annotations on the sketchbook's margins and in the Catalog, the piano variations and the vocal works on Italian texts are allowed to pass by, the numerous sketches for the Kreutzer are ignored, and the irregular opus number for the Bagatelle is

---

[7] W. Lenz, *Beethoven*, Bd III. Hamburg, 1860.

[8] W. Lenz, p. 222.

[9] W. Lenz.

used. Involuntarily, the question arises: are not the author of the Catalog and the annotator one and the same? Just so: a comparison of the notations with an unpublished document reveals that they belong to the same hand, and this document is a letter of April 6th (no year indicated) written by Wilhelm von Lenz.[10]

Of course, the annotations appear to be earlier than the published Catalog. Lenz became acquainted with this sketchbook before 1860. And in the Catalog he indicates its location at that time: "the musical library of Count Wielhorsky in Petersburg."[11]

One of the outstanding Russian Beethoven scholars in the first half of the past century, Mixail Jur'evic Viel'gorskij (1787-1856) used to play in his youth, under his father's direction, the viola part in Beethoven's early quartets, and in his twentieth year, stopping in Vienna on a return trip to Russia from France — by way of Austria — he had the honor to meet Beethoven personally. "The Count, having just met Beethoven, writes A. N. Serov of Viel'gorskij, "did not shrink from him, but entered into a conversation on music... he had the incredible — for us — privilege to hear the improvisations of the greatest genius of symphonic music in the world.[12]

According to Schiller's account (cited by Thayer), Viel'gorskij was one of the very few who were present at the first performance of the Pastoral Symphony (Vienna, December 1808).[13]

Based on Viel'gorskij's personal acquaintance with Beethoven, N. F. Findejzen once suggested that the Beethoven manuscript could have been in the Viel'gorskij collection from the year 1808. "It is possible, he writes, that from this period stems the acquisition of the musical manuscript found in the legacy of M. Viel'gorskij.[14]

Of course, the meetings with Beethoven, the conversations with him about art, and the hearing of his improvisations did not fail to impress Viel'gorskij. When he returned to

---

[10] Letter to M. J. Viel'gorskij in the manuscript section of the Lenin State Museum of the USSR, f. 48, p. 51, No.8.

[11] W. Lenz, *Beethoven*, Bd III, p. 221.

[12] A. N. Serov, Afterword "ot perevodčika ("Translator's Note") to W. Lenz's article "Graf Mixail Jur'evič Viel'gorskij," *Muzykal'nyj i teatral'nyj vestnik*, 1856, No. 51, pp. 918-919.

[13] Thayer, Bd III, p. 83.

[14] N. Findejzen, "Graf Mixail Jur'evič Viel'gorskij (k pjatidesjatiletiju so dnja smerti ["to the 50th anniversary of his death"])," *Russkaja muzykal'naja gazeta*, 1906, No. 35-36, p. 752.

Russia, he became an indefatigable propagandist for the creator of the Pastoral Symphony. For example, an important place in the history of Russian Beethoveniana is occupied by the cycle of concerts, known as the "Louisian" concerts (named for Viel'gorskij's wife, Luiza), which took place in the winter of 1822-1823 in the village of Pateyevok in Kyrsk province. In this cycle many works of western European music were performed. Beethoven was represented by almost all his largest symphonic works written before 1820.[15]

---

[15] Below is given a table of the performances of Beethoven's compositions in the "Louisian" concert cycle, which has been taken from the diary of Luiza Viel'gorskij-Biron (Manuscript Division of the Lenin State Library of the USSR, f. 48, p. 51, No.9).

Title of Composition	Dates of Performance				
	Dec 1822	Jan 1823	Feb 1823	Mar 1823	Apr 1823
Symphony No. 2	-	-	-	20	-
Eroica Symphony	-	-	-	-	5
Symphony No. 4	14, 26	16, 17	-	-	14, 15
Symphony No. 5	-	18, 26	-	-	13
Pastoral Symphony	-	21	6	-	-
Symphony No. 7	-	-	-	-	7
Wellington's Victory	-	2, 15	-	-	-
Overture to *Fidelio*	-	-	3	-	13
Overture to *Egmont*	-	-	9	-	-

However important the role his personal acquaintance with Beethoven played in his life and work, Viel'gorskij could not have received the Heiligenstadt sketchbook directly as a result of his visit to Vienna in 1808. Findejzen's opinion was put forth without regard to the contents of the manuscript. It is difficult to assume that in 1808 Beethoven would part with the drafts of compositions not only unpublished, but still unperformed: the oratorio Op. 85 (first published in 1811), the Terzett Op. 116 (first performed 1814, first published 1826), the Bagatelle Op. 119 (first published 1823), and the duet *Nei giorni tuoi felici* (neither performed nor published in Beethoven's lifetime). Naturally the Heiligenstadt sketchbook came into Russia only after Beethoven's death.

The information in the second volume of Nohl's Beethoven (Leipzig, 1867) is also based on an evident misunderstanding (though of a somewhat different nature). Referring to Nottebohm's accomplishment two years earlier — the publication of the Kessler sketchbook — and enumerating the compositions in it, Nohl added on his own: "As luck would have it, Nottebohm described not long ago a sketchbook now sold into Russia, from which it is evident what sort of ideas were then filling Beethoven's mind" (he is talking about Beethoven's stay in Heiligenstadt in the summer of 1802).[16]

Here three mistakes are combined at the same time: First of all, the works represented in the Kessler sketchbook described by Nottebohm were composed by Beethoven not at Heiligenstadt, but before his arrival there. Secondly, the Kessler sketchbook was not at all in Russia. Finally, Gustav Nottebohm not only did not describe the Heiligenstadt sketchbook, but, judging from his articles, did not even see the book.

Overture to *Coriolanus*	-	15	-	-	-
Quintet (arrangement of a septet)	-	19	-	-	-
Oratorio Op. 85 (Introduction and 3 numbers)	-	18	-	-	-

[16] L. Nohl, Beethoven, Ed II, p. 155.

Nohl simply confused two earlier sketchbooks.[17]

Afterwards, visiting Petersburg, Nohl himself discovered this contusion and in subsequent editions of his three-volume work, he withdrew the sentence about the sale of the sketchbook. Moreover, he published an article in 1874 in which he pointed out that the Beethoven sketchbook in Russia resembles that described by Nottebohm only in external appearance. In the article, incidentally, it is stated that "the book belongs to the oldest daughter of Count Wielhorsky, the wife of Senator Wenewitinow (that is, A. M. Viel'gorskij-Venevitinova) and that "in the Wielhorsky library it is catalogued under the number 64."[18]

Nohl's important correction, made in a special scientific article, did not reach, however, that circle of readers who knew only the Beethoven book described in the 1867 edition. And in the 1890's this first edition was translated into Russian, and a copy fell into the hands of the next owner of the Heiligenstadt sketchbook — the grandson of M. J. Viel'gorskij and the son of A. M. Venevitinova — the archaeologist and composer M. A. Venevitinov (at this time, the Heiligenstadt sketchbook was already in Moscow, where Venevitinov held the post of Director of the Publicnyj and Rumjancevskij Museum). Having read in Nohl's work the information that the book sold into Russia was described by Nottebohm, and unaware that Nohl himself had already retracted that statement, Venevitinov turned to S. I. Tanejev (the eminent Russian musicologist) with a request to

---

[17] Nohl's oversight is partly understandable for specific reasons. The complicated and often jumbled nature of transactions regarding the purchase and sale of Beethoven autographs may be seen from the following instance: On March 20, 1853, the owner of the largest private German collection of musical autographs, Aloys Fuchs, died. His legacy did not pass entire into any one library; a portion of the Beethoven manuscripts which he owned went to the pianist Josef Fischhof, and upon that person's death, to the bookseller Friedlander, and from him to the Royal Library in Berlin in 1859.

In 1921 W. Altmann published information from which it could be concluded that Friedlander had not sold to the Berlin Library all the Beethoven autographs which had belonged to Fischhof (*cf.* W. Altmann, "Die Musikabteilung der Preussischen Staatsbibliothek in Berlin," *Zeitschrift für Musikwissenschaft*, 1921, Heft 7, p. 430). But in 1953 — exactly 100 years after Fuchs's death — G. Edelmann and L. Rojzman discovered in Moscow — in the archives of N. B. Jusupov — a Beethoven manuscript...with Fischhof's stamp on it (*cf. Sovetskaja muzyka*, 1953, No.5, p. 76). Is it any wonder that Nohl could confuse which manuscripts had been sold into Russia, and which had not?

[18] L. Nohl, p. 96.

borrow, "if only for a few hours," Nottebohm's volume which Nohl cited.[19]

When he received the book from Tanejev, Venevitinov, who was a good musician, easily discovered Nohl's mistake. On the next day he again wrote Tanejev: "Isn't there another source from which I might find out about the sketchbook which I have?"[20]

By the letters of Venevitinov, still another version of Viel'gorskij's acquisition of the Beethoven manuscript is proved false — the version, rather widely circulated, whose author appears to have been the fairly well-known O. A. Smirnova-Rosset. In her house, as she related it, there was once supposed to have been a meeting of Alexander Pushkin and Mixail Viel'gorskij with a certain Madame Hirt. Learning that Madame Hirt was a pupil of Beethoven's, Pushkin and Viel'gorsklj bombarded her with inquiries about his deafness, his melancholy, his peculiar ideas, and about the blind girl for whom he composed the Moonlight Sonata." O. A. Smirnova asserted that at the time of this conversation "Madame Hirt promised Viel'gorskij the Beethoven manuscript."[21]
Such a meeting may have taken place, and it is possible that Madame Hirt actually did promise Viel'gorskij some kind of Beethoven manuscript. But could it have been the Heiligenstadt sketchbook, could it have come into Viel'gorskij's possession while Alexander Pushkin was alive? [Pushkin died in 1837. — Ed.]

We think a negative answer is given by Venevitinov's letters to Tanejev. For Venevitinov personally knew his grandfather, Mixail Viel'gorskij, more intimately than anyone else, and he studied his archives and had a particular knowledge of all the family legends. If the sketchbook had come to Viel'gorskij in those years when such a meeting could have taken place, Venevitinov could hardly have attached importance to Nohl's remark about a "recent sale," and he would scarcely have begun to search for an account of the book in the works of his contemporary Nottebohm, who had never been in Russia.

Of course, it would be desirable if the number which the Heiligenstadt sketchbook received, not only in Viel'gorskij's library, but in the auction at Kohlmarkt as well [This

---

[19] Letter of March 1, 1900, in the Tchaikovsky House Museum in Klina, S. I. Tanejev Archives (V, v[11] No. 759).
[20] Letter of March 2, 1900, in the Tchaikovsky House Museum in Klina, S. I. Tanejev Archives (V, v[11] No. 760).
[21] From the article of M. P. Aleksejev, "Russkie vstreči i svjazi Betxovena" ["Russian encounters and contacts of Beethoven"] in Sbornik (Collection), *Russkaya kniga o Beetxovena*, Moscow 1927, p. 87.

refers to the sale of Beethoven's belongings after his death. — Ed.], could be used to shed light on who bought the book at the auction, and who sold it or made a present of it to Viel'gorskij. For at the time of the auction in Vienna, Maurer was close to Viel'gorskij. So was Hunke. Both left Vienna taking with them Beethoven manuscripts. Could Gräffer have forgotten to take down their names when he declared sold the "Books of Notes" designated by Nos. 12, 19, 22, and 27? (The names of the buyers of these numbers remain unknown as well.)

Unfortunately there is no information permitting an answer to that question, either in the printed materials or in the archives. It does not help to turn to the inheritance or the auction list, which was drawn up soon after Beethoven's death and which is now kept in the Beethovenhaus Museum in Bonn.

Thus it is necessary, in the matter in question, to confine oneself to the suggesting of only a period of time when Viel'gorskij could have received the Heiligenstadt sketchbook, and to refrain from the fixing of an exact date and circumstances of acquisition. Excluding consideration of the unfounded versions criticized above, one may arrive at a determination of the period on the basis of the following reasoning.
It is known that Lenz wrote two main works on Beethoven. The first, *Beethoven and his Three Styles*, was published in Petersburg in 1852, and the second — *Beethoven* — in Kassel and Hamburg in 1856-1860. In both works there is a "Catalog of Beethoven's Works, and in particular a paragraph devoted to Op. 85. In the first edition of the Catalog there is no mention of the sketchbook belonging to Viel'gorskij, but the second edition makes such a mention.

Lenz was a close acquaintance of Viel'gorskij; he called him his "spiritual father"[22] and had already in the 1800's come to work in Viel'gorskij's library. If the Heiligenstadt sketchbook had come into that library earlier than the middle of the century, Lenz surely would have mentioned it in his work, timed for the twenty-fifth year after Beethoven's death.

Something else is still more crucial, a letter of Lenz's to Viel'gorskij on the 6th of April (no year indicated) devoted entirely to the symphonies of Beethoven. But in speaking of the *Eroica*, Lenz constructs no history of its composition in terms of the sketches. In the second edition of the Catalog, however, he attempts to fix the time of the

---

[22] Letter to F. Liszt on January 21, 1857. *Russkaja muzykal'naya gazeta*, 1896, No. 7, p. 723.

Symphony's composition on the basis of the sketches in the book belonging to Viel'gorskij.[23] This clearly shows that at the moment of writing the letter Lenz had still not seen the Heiligenstadt sketchbook, although he was in closest contact with Viel'gorskij in matters concerning Beethoven scholarship. The letter, judging from its contents, could not have been written earlier than the first appearance of the Catalog.

And so, the Heiligenstadt sketchbook came into the collection of Mixail Viel'gorskij between 1853 and 1856. It is possible that it came into the collection after the death of Viel'gorskij himself. But in any case — not later than 1859.

* * *

At the end of the nineteenth and the beginning of the twentieth centuries, a series of articles and notes devoted to a description of the Viel'gorskij-Venevitinov collections appeared in Russian journals. Very likely the most significant of these articles is that serialized in the April 1900 issues (nos. 15-17) of the Russkaja Muzykal'naja Gazeta. This article is entitled "80 and 60 Years Ago." The author was S. V. Smolenskij, a well-known musicologist and researcher in Russian music.

Smolenskij touches twice upon the Beethoven manuscript — in the beginning and at the end of the article — not once, however, naming Beethoven himself. "I permit myself," wrote Smolenskij, "to put aside information about one amazing manuscript until such time when more detailed study of this major document will make it possible to write an account worthy of it, and perhaps to have it appear in print." And further: ...there is a varied collection [at Venevitinov's] of portraits, manuscripts, and, among others, one genuine rarity, about which I remain silent for the time being."[24]

In concealing from the readers of the journal the contents of the "genuine rarity," Smolenskij gave them advance notice of the possibility of its appearance in print. On what did he base this information? The answer to that question is contained in letters of S. I. Tanejev and M. P. Beljaev which are kept in the museum of the Tchaikovsky House in Klina and in the Glinka Museum in Moscow.

On February 28, 1900, M. A. Venevitinov invited S. I. Tanejev and S. V. Smolenskij to his home in order to acquaint them with the Beethoven manuscript. On that same day

---

[23] Basing himself on Ries' erroneous dating of the oratorio Op. 85, Lenz mistakenly dates the sketchbook in the Viel'gorskij collection as belonging to 1800, and not to 1802.

[24] pp. 426 and 477 of the April issues.

in Tanejev's diary appears the following entry determining the contents of the manuscript which he viewed: "A sketchbook of Beethoven's... Sketches for the Sonata in E-Flat, variations, many things with text (I think it is Christus am Oelberg). He [Venevitinov] did not have anything against suggesting to Beljaev that it be published."[25]

Tanejev did not confine himself to a single visit, but returned to Venevitinov's on the 9th, 13th, and 23rd of March. He did not have a copy of the score of Beethoven's oratorio in his own library, and — before one of the visits to Venevitinov — dropped in on G. L. Katuar in order to obtain one. On March 19th Tanejev approached M. P. Beljaev by letter.

"In the last few days very unusual circumstances impel me to write you... In Moscow there has been found a personal notebook of his [Beethoven's] sketches. It belongs to the Director of the Rumyancevskij Museum, Mixail Alekseyevič Venevitinov. The notebook came to him from his grandfather Mixail Jur'evič Viel'gorskij, and there can be no doubt as to its genuineness. In it are numerous sketches for the Sonata in E-Flat, Op. 31, for the Piano Variations and Fugue Op. 35, serving afterwards for the finale of the *Eroica* Symphony, and very many fragments with German text, in all probability related to the oratorio Christ on the Mount of Olives (in a few days I shall verify this). When I saw this jewel I first of all thought how wonderful it would be to publish it in facsimile, and I determined to persuade you to that end... If it were to fall to the lot of a Russian publisher to acquaint the musical world with a genuine Beethoven sketchbook, where one could see how he worked, in what order his thoughts replaced one another, and precisely the fact that he would deem it necessary to discard or change something else, then how splendid it would be!"[26]

Beljaev did not carry out the request, motivating his refusal on the ground that in the task of publishing he did not consider as a part of his work the printing of the music of foreign composers.[27] Tanejev was deeply grieved. "I am greatly sorry," he wrote to Beljaev on April 6, 1900, "that you do not want to make an exception even for this composer. Beethoven cannot at all be correctly regarded as a German composer. He

[25] V, v[11] No. 37 in the Tanejev Archives of the museum of the Tchaikovsky House in Klina.

[26] Letter of S. I. Tanejev to M. P. Belyaev on March 19, 1900, in the Glinka State Central Museum of Musical Culture, in the M. P. Belyaev section (f. 41, No. 470).

[27] *Cf.* the letter from M. P. Belyaev to S. I. Tanejev on March 29, 1900, in the Tanejev archives of the Museum of the Tchaikovsky House in Klina (V, v[11]No. 615).

belongs to the whole world, and in that number, to us — to Russians.[28] But Beljaev continued to remain deaf to Tanejev's arguments. The book was not published.

Twelve days after Tanejev wrote the above letter, on April 18, 1900, M. A. Venevitinov became seriously ill. In the course of the following eighteen months he was paralyzed, and in September 1901 he died. At this time the Heiligenstadt sketchbook drops out of sight for a while from the musical world. Although Venevitinov's library and a part of the family archives were donated by the Ruajancevskij Museum by two of the heirs, there is no information in the museum's records of any Beethoven manuscript. In 1906 the editor of the Russkaja Muzykal'naja Gazeta, N. F. Findejzen, came forth with the statement in print that, of the Beethoven manuscript in the Vlel'gorskij legacy, to which "S. V. Smolenskij alluded... from that time on [that is, from 1900] nothing further is known."[29] In fact, no documents about the sketchbook's location between 1902 and 1911 have been discovered.

The mysterious disappearance of the sketchbook became known abroad: in the 1920's and 1930's it was considered lost.[30] Meanwhile, the book was in fact found again after the Great October Socialist Revolution. It remained in one of the Moscow state archives, and as far back as 1927 an employee of the archives, A. Semënlj, compiled (from Lenz's notes) a brief list of the Beethoven compositions represented in it. In 1939, upon the request of Professor A. B. Goldenweiser — at the time the Director of the Moscow Conservatory — the book was transferred to the Conservatory Library, and in 1943 to the State Central Museum of Musical Culture.[31] At present the Heiligenstadt sketchbook

---

[28] Letter of S. I. Tanejev to M. P. Belyaev on April 6, 1900, in the M. P. Belyaev section of the Glinka State Central Museum of Musical Culture (f. 41, No. 473).

[29] N. F. Findejzen, "Graf Mixail Jur'evič Viel'gorskij," *Russkaja muzykal'naja gazeta*, 1906, Nos. 35-36, p. 752.

[30] For example, the well-known Swiss Beethoven scholar, Willy Hess, in the foreword to his edition of the duet *Nei giorni*, wrote that "the sketchbook which was formerly in the possession of Count Wielhorsky is now lost" (*cf.* the Eulenburg Miniature Score of the duet, published at Leipzig in 1939).

[31] In the second issue of *Sovetskaja muzyka* for the year 1940, in the "Xronika" ("Events") section (p. 94), there is a brief notice to the effect: "A Beethoven notebook has come to the Moscow Conservatory Library from one of the Moscow state archives. At the present time a photographic reproduction, in actual size, of the notebook is being prepared. When this has been made, detailed musicological study of the manuscript will begin." The preparation of the edition was entrusted to the musicologist G. M. Van'kovič. It was planned to include it in the collection being prepared by

forms a part of the musical treasury of the past, guarded by the people, and adorns the specially created Beethoven section in the Glinka Museum.

[End of Haley 1966 translation of Fishman (1962), vol. III, pp. 13-22.]

---

the library for the 75th anniversary of the Moscow Conservatory (September 1, 1941).

As is known, the war with fascist Germany, which began on June 22, 1941, prevented the carrying out of all these plans. The systematic study of the Heiligenstadt sketchbook could begin only after the war had been over for a number of years. At that time the transcribing of the book was included in the research plan of the Manuscript Archive Division of the Glinka Museum. The first (preliminary) results of this work were published in the journal *Sovetskaja muzyka*, 1953, No. 3 (*cf.* the article "Neopublikovannaja rykopis' èskizov sonaty Betxovena" ["An Unpublished Manuscript of Sketches for a Beethoven Sonata"]), and in the second volume of the annual *Voprosy muzykovanija* (Moscow, 1956, pp. 525-561).

Appendix B: A Contemporary Account of Madame Viganò

A contemporary, Caroline Pichler, wrote of Madam Viganò (Pichler 1844, vol. 1, 205f.): "Nature was imitated to the truest degree. Flesh-colored tricots covered arms and legs, but the dancers were scarcely clothed: in the so-called *pas de deux en rose* Madam Viganò wore over the tricot that covered her entire body nothing but three or four fluttering skirts of crèpe, each one shorter than the other and bound all together with a sash of dark brown ribbon around the middle of her body. This sash was actually, therefore, the only piece of clothing that covered her, because the crèpe hid nothing, and during her dance these skirts—or actually, furbelows—flew all the way up and treated the public to the sight of the dancer's entire body in flesh-colored tricot, which looked like skin, thus seemingly naked. This struck me as outrageously impudent, but I must admit that the movements of this artist were enchantingly graceful, the play of her features was full of expression (she was moreover very pretty), and her pantomimes were masterly. The sensation made here by this woman, and by the ballets which her husband presented, was enormous." ("Die Natur wurde auf treueste nachgeahmt. Fleischfarbene Trikots umhüllten Arme und Beine, die Tänzer und Tänzerinnen waren kaum bekleidet, ja in dem sogenannten rosenfarben Pas de deux hatte Mad. Vigano über den Trikot, der ihren ganzen Leib umgab, nichts an als drei bis vier flatternde Röckchen von Krepp, immer eins kürzer wie das andere und alle zusammen mit einem Gürtel von dunkelbraunem Band um die mitte des Leibes festgebunden. Eigentlich war also dieses Band das einzige Kleidungstück, das sie bedeckte, denn der Krepp verhüllte nichts, im Tanze flogen oft noch diese Röckchen oder eigentlich Falbulas hoch empor und ließen dem Publikum den ganzen Körper der Tänzerin in fleischfarbenem Trikot, der die Haut nachahmte, also scheinbar ganz entblößt sehen. Mir kam das empörend frech vor, dennoch mußte ich gestehen, daß die Bewegungen dieser Künstlerin hinreißend anmutig, ihr Mienenspiel voll Ausdruck (sie war noch überdies sehr hübsch), ihre Pantominen meisterhaft waren. Die Sensation, welche diese Frau und die Ballette, welche ihr Mann aufführte, hier machten, war ungeheuer.")

Appendix C:

A New Translation of Ritorni's Remarks on Viganò's Ballet
Die Geschöpfe des Prometheus

Plates 8-9: Pages 47-50 from Ritorni (1838)

— 47 —

ricco alunno fa novella festa. Nel quint' atto è attaccata una taglia dell' Usurpatore contro Cloüilde. Agognano i Zingari a guadagnarla, ma la Principessa è nuovamente soccorsa dalle femmine, e da Alessandro, e infine più efficacemente dall'armi di Ruggero, che riconosce il figlio, e vuole, ma invano, staccarlo dall'amata e amante Zingara novella, la quale poi è riconosciuta e palesata da Ambasciatori giunti di Salerno, che recano: il Tiranno esser abbattuto, ed essa libera possieditrice del trono paterno. Finiva con balli l'azione che n'aveva già dovizia in più luoghi.

XXVII. GLI UOMINI DI PROMETEO ossia *La forza della musica e della danza*. Incalzato dalla fulminante ira del Cielo, che dà luogo a fragoroso musical preludio, vien Prometeo pel bosco correndo verso le sue statue della creta, cui frettoloso accosta al cuore la fiaccola celeste. Mentr' egli affaticato, affannato, compita l'opera, s'abbandona su un sasso, quelle acquistan vita e movimento, e diventano in fatto, quali eran in apparenza, un uomo ed una donna (Salvatore stesso e la brava Casentini). Prometeo riscuotendosi li guarda con giubilo, li invita a sè con paterno amore, ma non può destare in essi alcun sentimento che mostri uso di ragione: anzi quelli, lasciandosi cader in terra indolentemente, piucchè a lui rivolgonsi ad un'alta pianta: (vorrebbe ciò per avventura indicare quella delle ghiande, che furono indispensabile alimento agli uomini primi?) Ritorna egli alle carezze ed alle persuasive, ma coloro che di uomini non hanno la miglior

— 48 —

parte, la ragione, non intendono le sue parole, e sen'infastidiscono, e coll'inetto loro aggirarsi tentano andar più lunge. Dolente il Titano prova ancor le minaccie, e nulla giovando, sdegnato pensa perfino a dover distruggere quell'opera sua; ma voce superna internamente ne lo ritrae, sicchè torna al primo affetto, e mostrando nuovo disegno esser nato nella sua mente, seco entrambi, afferrati, altrove strascina.

L'atto secondo è nel Parnaso. Apollo, le Muse, le Grazie, Bacco e Pane con seguito, Orfeo, Anfione, Arione, uomini nascituri, e con anacronismo introdotti. Un bel quadro di queste poetiche figure mostra all'aprir della scena la corte di Apollo. Notisi che il Coreografo non vuol qui nè musica nè danza specialmente, onde allorchè queste verranno adoperate poi come mezzi particolari, se ne conosca il loro novello intervenimento: savia avvertenza in ogni simile caso! Vien Prometeo, presentando al Nume i figli suoi, perchè gli piaccia farli capaci dell'arti e delle scienze. Al cenno di Febo, Euterpe, secondata da Anfione, mettesi a suonare, ed alle loro modulazioni i due giovinetti cominciano dar segno di ragione, di riflessione, di veder le bellezze della natura, di sentir umani affetti. Arione ed Orfeo rafforzano l'armonia colle loro cetere, ed ultimamente il Nume secoloro. I Candidati agitansi quà e là, e giunti avanti Prometeo, conoscon in lui l'oggetto di lor riconoscenza e amore, e gli si prostrano, e seco confondono gli affettuosi amplessi. Allora avvanza Tersicore colle Grazie, e Bacco co'

93

suoi Baccanti, che menano una danza eroica (più propria del seguito di Marte) nella quale i figli di Prometeo, non reggendo ommai agli stimoli della gloria, dato dipiglio all'armi, voglionsi mischiare. Ma Melpomene allora, recatasi inmezzo, a' Giovanetti attoniti rappresenta una tragica scena, facendo vedere col suo pugnale come morte termini i giorni dell'uomo. Raccappricciandone essi, volgesi al Padre confuso, e lo rimprovera, aver fatti nascere que' miseri a tali calamità, nè crede punirlo soverchiamente colla morte, il perchè, invan rattenuta da' pietosi figli, di pugnale l'uccide. Rompe quel lutto Talia con una giuocosa scena, ponendo sua maschera avanti'l volto de' due piangenti, mentre Pane, alla testa de' Fauni, comicamente danzanti, torna a vita l'estinto Titano, e così fra danze festive termina la favola. Questo scioglimento non corrisponde alla gravità del subbietto. Non conviene a divinità allegorica uccidere, nè a Melpomene dar morte vera, ma imitar vere catastrofi sanguinose. Perchè non rappresentar piuttosto, dopo il tragico fine dell'uomo, l'immortal vita dell'anima, mercè l'apoteosi di Prometeo, cui conveniva ad Apollo, nume dell'azione, innalzar a vita immortale? Ma il presente sembra essere stato uno scenico divertimento, in cui non si volle impiegare vastità di scena, macchine e spettacolo.

L'idea di così piccol componimento, inventato in onore dell'amor che per la musica aveva grandissimo l'imperatrice Maria Teresa seconda moglie dell'imperatore Francesco Secondo, è sublime, e

4

vedesi chiaramente questo che chiamerò ancora *Il piccolo Prometeo*, aver in sè quel germe che svilupposi poi nel gran Prometeo, col quale aprì Salvatore la serie de' capolavori suoi principali. Ma il second'atto difettosissimo, è, come apparisce, con poc'arte, nè miglior buongusto condotto.

XXVIII. De' I GIUOCHI ISTMICI non ho potuto per diligenze rintracciar il programma, e solamente da chi n'è appena ricordevole ho saputo, che l'argomento, tratto da un francese romanzo intitolato *Phrosine et Mélidor*, fu insinuato dalla suddetta imperatrice Maria Teresa, e venne pelle scene riportato a tema di greca antichità: diverso avviso da quello che prenderebbesi oggiddì. Una cospicua Donzella di Corinto è per diventare sposa a ragguardevole personaggio. Amava essa un valoroso giovin megarese; e il vede ne' giuochi vincitor di tutti i rivali suoi. Ammiravasi a quelli innestata una specie di giuoco de' palloni, nonsenz' aver il Viganò ritrovate autorità che non disconveniva ad un argomento dell' antichità; ed era piacevole (alcuni ne conservano dolce ricordanza eziandio fra l'obbivione di queste antiche cose) com' egli stesso, sostenendo la parte del protagonista vincitore, nel ballar un solo, gettava, raccoglieva, faceva in varie guise saltellar il suo pallone mentre menava difficilissime carole, e capriole rintrecciatissime, senzacchè quello cadesse in fallo giammai. Segue poi abboccamento de' due amanti in luogo remoto, ove sono sorpresi; ed in una zuffa il Megarese per salvar la propria vita, uccide il fratello dell'innamorata.

THE CREATURES OF PROMETHEUS

or

The power of music and dance

Pursued by the thundering wrath of heaven, which is depicted in a stormy musical prelude, Prometheus runs from the woods to his clay statues, and quickly touches the celestial torch to their hearts. As he sinks back on a stone, exhausted and breathless from fulfilling his task, the figures gain life and movement and become in fact what they appeared to be, a man and a woman (Salvatore himself and the splendid Casentini). Prometheus, rousing himself, looks at them with jubilation, and with paternal love bids them approach, but he cannot awaken in them any feeling that would show the use of reason: the humans rather, instead of turning to him, let themselves fall lazily to the ground near a tall tree. (Would [Salvatore], by chance, want this to signify the [oak] tree whose acorns were essential food for the first humans?) He turns to them again, with caresses and coaxing, but they, who lack man's better part—reason—do not understand his words, become annoyed, and wander about awkwardly, trying to go farther away. Afflicted, the Titan tries again with threats, which are of no use, and becoming incensed, he thinks he may even have to destroy his work; but a voice from on high internally pulls him back, so that his first affection [for them] returns, and having grabbed them both, showing a new plan has formed in his mind, he drags them offstage.

The second act is on Parnassus: [we see] Apollo, the Muses, the Graces, Bacchus and Pan with his train, Orpheus, and Amphion and Arion, [the latter] introduced anachronistically as men still to be born. The opening of the scene at Apollo's court shows a tableau vivant of these poetic figures. Notice that the choreographer especially desires neither music nor dancing at this point, so that when these particular media come to be used later, one does not notice that their presence is new: a word to the wise in all such cases! Prometheus enters and presents his children to the deity, that it might please him to make them skilled in the arts and sciences. On a gesture from Phoebus, Euterpe, followed by Amphion, start to play their instruments, and through their modulations the two young people begin to show signs of reason and reflection, to see the beauties of

95

nature, and to feel human affections. Arion and Orpheus reinforce the harmony with their lyres, and at the end the god himself joins in. The two pupils shake this way and that, and joined in front of Prometheus, they recognize in him the object of their gratitude and love, prostrate themselves, and embarrass him with affectionate embraces. Then Terpsichore comes forward with the Graces, and Bacchus and his Bacchantes, who lead a heroic dance (more fitting for the retinue of Mars), in which Prometheus' children, who by this time are unable to withstand the spurs to glory, and have taken up arms, willingly take part. But then Melpomene intervenes and stages a tragic scene for the astounded young ones, in which she makes them see with her dagger how death cuts short the days of man. While they stand horrified, she turns on their perplexed father, whom she rebukes for giving birth to wretches who face such a calamity, and considers it not out of line that he be punished by death himself. In vain the miserable children [try to] hold her back as she kills Prometheus with her dagger. Thalia interrupts the mourning with a merry scene, putting her mask in front of the faces of the two weeping ones. Next Pan, at the head of the fauns, and dancing comically, restores the dead Titan to life, and thus the tale ends amid festive dancing. This ending does not match the gravity of the subject. Murder does not become an allegorical goddess, nor is it for Melpomene to be the agent of actual death, but only to act out catastrophes filled with blood. Why not rather depict, after the tragic end of man, the immortal life of the soul, the mercy of the deification of Prometheus, whom it suited Apollo, the god of action, to raise to immortal life? The present [work], however, appears to have been a scenic divertimento, in which one does not want to employ a broad range of scenery, mechanical devices and spectacle.

The idea for this little composition, conceived in honor of that most splendid love for music borne by the empress Maria Theresa (second wife of Emperor Francis II), is sublime, and one sees clearly that this, which is still called 'The Little Prometheus', has in it the germ which developed later into the 'Big Prometheus', with which Salvatore began the series of his principal masterpieces. But the seriously defective second act is, it would seem, driven by little art, and by no better a sense of good taste.

(tr. by A. S. Haley)

Appendix D: Original (German) Text of a Contemporary Review of the Ballet

(From *Zeitung für die elegante Welt* I [April 1801], at 485-87; tr. *supra*, pp. 21-23.)

"Den Schluß der Vorstellungen auf unserem Hoftheater vor Ostern machte ein neues heroisch-allegorisches Ballet, in 2 Aufzügen: *Die Geschöpfe des Prometheus*, von der Erfindung und Ausführung des Herrn Salvatore Vigano, und in Musik gesetzt von Herrn van Beethoven. Das erste mal ward es zum Benefiz der berühmten Tänzerin, Demoiselle Casentini, gegeben. Der Inhalt davon ward in einem sehr sonderbaren Programme, vermutlich von einem der deutschen Sprache nicht so ganz kundigen Italiener, angekündigt.

"Prometheus entreißt die Menschen seiner Zeit der Unwissenheit, verfeinert sie durch Wissenschaft und Kunst und erhebt sie zur Sittlichkeit. Dies ist kürzlich das Sujet. So viel Würde und artistische Anlage es auch hatte, und so meisterhaft sich einige Tänzer, vorzüglich Herr Vigano selber auszeichneten, so gefiel es doch im Allgemein nicht. Am allerwenigsten Behagen konnte unser sinnliches Publikum daran finden, daß die Bühne von dem zweiten Auftritte des ersten Aufzuges an bis ganz ans Ende immer unverändert blieb. Die Handlung begann mit einem Donnerwetter. Das Theater stellte ein Wäldchen vor, in welchem sich zwei Kinder von Prometheus befanden. Plötzlich kam ihr Vater mit einer brennenden Fackel daher. (Wo, und mit welchem Feuer er sie angezündet, bekam der Zuschauer nicht zu sehen.) Nachdem er jedem Kinde das Feuer in die Brust gelegt, fingen diese sogleich an, steif und ohne Gestikulazion umherzutrippeln. (Dieser Auftritt dauerte etwas sehr lange und ennuyirte.) Nun führte Prometheus sie zum Apoll. Der Parnaß machten mit allen seinen Bewohnern eben nicht den angenehmsten Anblick. Die neun Musen blieben wie leblose Statuen so lange auf ihrem angewiesenen Platz, bis die Reihe zu tanzen auch an sie kam, und Apollo selbst saß auf der höchsten Spitze des Berges, stets unbeweglich. Vielleicht machte eben dieser Anblick zu wenig Eindruck auf den Künstlergeist unserer beliebten *Casentini*, indem sie, von ihrem Vater dem Musen-Gott vorgestellt, so gar keine Theilnahme äußerte, und ihren Blick mit auffallender Gleichgültigkeit sogleich auf andere Gegenstände abschweifen ließ. Denn daß sie die einem solchen Publicum schuldige Hochachtung, besonders in einem Ballete, das ihr über baare 4000 Gulden eintrug, blos aus übler Laune sollte hintangesetzt haben, kann man sich doch nicht bereden. Gewiß aber würde sie, blos mit etwas mehr Anstrengung – wiewohl eine Casentini nie schlecht tanzen kann – das Ballet weit mehr anziehend gemacht haben.

"Auch die Musik entsprach der Erwartung nicht ganz, ohneractet sie nicht *gemeine* Vorzüge besitzt. Ob Herr van Beethoven bei der Einheit – um nicht Einförmigkeit der Handlung zu sagen, das leisten konnte, was ein Publicum, wie das hiesige, fordert, will ich unentschieden lassen. Daß er aber für ein Ballet zu gelehrt und mit zu wenig Rücksicht auf den Tanz schrieb, ist wohl keinem Zweifel unterworfen. Alles ist für ein Divertissement, was denn doch das Ballet eigentlich seyn soll, zu groß angelegt, und bey dem Mangel an dazu passenden Situazionen, hat es mehr Bruchstück als Ganzes bleiben müssen. Dies fängt schon mit der Ouvertüre an. Bei jeder größern Oper würde sie an ihrer Stelle seyn, und einer bedeutenden Wirkung nicht verfehlen; hier aber steht sie an ihrer unrechten Stelle. Die kriegerischen Tänze und das Solo der Demoiselle Casentini mögten übrigens wohl dem Compositeur am besten gelungen seyn. Bei dem Tanz des Pans will man einige Reminiszenzen aus anderen Ballets gefunden haben. Allein, mich dünkt, es geschieht Herrn van B. hierin zuviel, zumal da nur seine Neider ihm eine ganz vorzügliche Originalität absprechen können, durch welche freylich er öfter seinen Zuschauern den Reiz sanfter gefälliger Harmonien entzieht."

Appendix E: The Errors in Thayer's Chronology

For ease of reference in the critique that follows, I give here again the quote from Thayer that appears in the text at Note 90 (pp. 32-33):

"Is it possible that Court Councilor Lenz confused studies for the piano variations Op. 35 with those for the finale of the *Eroica?* If not, then this sketchbook offers us a very interesting clarification: that in the spring [of 1801] Beethoven worked the *Prometheus-*theme into a set of variations for orchestra; that in autumn he changed his mind and used the same sketches in the piano variations; that in the winter he transformed the theme into a contredanse (perhaps to make it more well-known?), and finally in 1803 he returned to his original idea of the *Sinfonia Eroica* and elaborated the orchestral variations as the finale, while the funeral march [also described by von Lenz as among the sketches], took the place of the slow movement."

In so writing, Thayer was misled by the errors of a number of earlier authors. Begin with the mistake of von Lenz, who, in describing the sketchbook, placed it in his Beethoven catalog under op. 85 (*Christus am Oelberge*), undoubtedly because it contained a large number of sketches for the oratorio. Von Lenz, however, took it from Schindler that Beethoven had sketched the oratorio while staying in the summer *of 1800* at Hetzendorf, because, as Schindler assured his readers, Beethoven himself had pointed out to Schindler (in 1823!) the very spot under a branching oak tree where he sat while working—allegedly in that year—on his oratorio. (Schindler 1845, 46-47.) This erroneous date was unfortunately corroborated by Beethoven's pupil Ferdinand Ries, who wrote in his own biography of Beethoven that when he arrived in Vienna *in 1800,* he found Beethoven hard at work on the music for the oratorio. (Wegeler/Ries, 75; Eng. tr. (Noonan 1988), at 65.)

Thayer's independent research, however, had convinced him that Beethoven spent the summer of 1800 at Unterdöbling, a suburb of Vienna, and that he had stayed at Hetzendorf in the summer of 1801. (Thayer, vol. 2, 103-04, and 131-32.) From other evidence, it appeared to Thayer that Ries was also mistaken in his memory, and that he had not arrived in Vienna until 1801. (Thayer, vol. 2, 161-63. On possible revisions to Ries's chronology, *see* Zanden 2005.)

By the time he wrote the passage above, Schindler (in his third edition) had also changed the date of the stay in Hetzendorf from 1800 to 1801. (Schindler 1860, at 90; Eng. tr. [MacArdle (ed.) 1996] at 99.) So Thayer now read von Lenz's description of what was in the sketchbook to relate to the summer and fall of 1801. He noted that von Lenz had reported that there was a reference to a funeral march, and what he thought were sketches for the *Eroica* finale, which preceded those for the oratorio (*see* Appendix A, p. 79). Thayer tied this observation in with what he knew about the dates when the ballet was first performed and when the contredanses were performed to arrive at the following ordering:

March 1801 – First performance of *Prometheus*, so the work was complete by then

Spring 1801 – Sketches for the *Eroica* finale in the Wielhorsky sketchbook, plus an indication of the funeral march, which precede the sketches for the oratorio (mistakenly thought to be written in summer 1801)

Fall 1801 – Based on Gustav Nottebohm's description published in 1865 of the op. 35 sketches that appear in the Kessler sketchbook (N 1865, 32), Thayer asserts that Beethoven "changed his mind" at this time and used his previous work on the finale as the basis for the piano variations, op. 35.

Winter 1801 – As Thayer is aware, Beethoven scored the collection of contredanses at this time for the forthcoming ball season in Vienna, and so he surmises that Beethoven decided to use the dances as a vehicle to make better known the theme which he was planning for further works. (Thayer, vol. 2, at 393.)

This chronology is possible only because Thayer has accepted spring 1801 as the date for the Wielhorsky sketchbook, and thus has it precede the Kessler sketchbook, which Beethoven began in approximately October 1801. In point of fact, however, the Wielhorsky sketchbook followed *immediately after* Kessler, as Ludwig Nohl concluded in his 1874 report (Nohl 1874, at 95-101), when he saw that what von Lenz had described as *Eroica* finale sketches were in fact the finishing sketches for op. 35, which Beethoven offered to his publisher in October 1802. (BGA No. 107, dated October 18, 1802.)

Appendix F: How TDR's Errors Misled Later Scholarship

A little more history supplies a probable explanation for the adherence to an improbable theory in subsequent Beethoven scholarship (namely, that the contredanse came before the ballet). As noted above, Herman Deiters took it upon himself to revise Thayer's hypothetical chronology, based solely on internal evidence, and not on any examination of the autographs or the sketches. When Deiters' successor, Hugo Riemann, took over Thayer's biography, he elaborated on Deiters' thesis: based on a thorough analytic study of the ballet score and the Symphony, he came to view all of the music for *Prometheus* as a "Variationenwerk" (set of variations) that, in effect, was a precursor of the *Eroica* finale. (Riemann 1909-10.) In doing so, he agreed with Deiters' view that the contredanse had to come first, because otherwise the increasingly elaborate use which Beethoven made of such a simple theme could not be viewed in a linear fashion. (*Id.* at 19; TDR II, pp. 422-24. Fishman mistakenly asserts that Riemann parted ways with Deiters on this point. Fishman, vol. III, at 54, n 2.)

The position staked out by Deiters and Riemann was adopted uncritically by Paul Mies in his influential study of Beethoven's progressive development of the theme, which signaled his viewpoint in its title: *"Beethovens Werke uber seinen Kontretanz in Es-Dur"*. (Mies 1953-54. Mies, however, ignores Riemann's indication, through the editorially inserted initials as shown earlier, that the argument for placing the contredanse first originated with Deiters, and attributes the idea solely to Riemann.)

One year later came the publication of the definitive catalog of Beethoven's works (KH), authored by Georg Kinsky and completed after his death by Hans Halm. Coincidentally, it appeared to corroborate the Deiters-Riemann-Mies position when it cited the *Entstehungszeit* (time of composition) for the twelve contredanses (WoO 14) as "1800-01" (KH 450), and for the ballet, "1800 und Anfang 1801" (KH 102). Kinsky-Halm makes clear in its following notes that the WoO 14 date "1800" is a compromise to allow for those earlier-composed contredanses (Nos. 3, 4, 8 and 12) which Nottebohm indicated were written "at the latest" by 1800. (Nottebohm 1868, at 198.) Nevertheless, it permitted the inference that it agreed with the Deiters-Riemann hypothesis when it asserted that Beethoven "transferred" (*"übernahm"*) Nos. 7 and 11 into his "simultaneously" (*"gleichzeitig"*) composed ballet. To "transfer" the dances means that they must have been composed previously; asserting that the composition of the ballet was *"gleichzeitig"* with their composition creates needless ambiguity and confusion, which has misled scholars ever since.

Subsequent Beethoven scholars, such as Elliot Forbes, Harry Goldschmidt, Lewis Lockwood, Christopher Reynolds, William Kinderman, Carl Dahlhaus, and others, have uncritically adopted the position that the contredanse preceded the ballet, based on a citation (when they give one) to TDR and the ambiguous confirmation supplied by Kinsky-Halm. Thus, Elliot Forbes repeats the ambiguous dating of KH and states that "Beethoven also used two of these dances . . . in his ballet . . ." (Thayer-Forbes, 297-98); Harry Goldschmidt, while pointing out that Prometheus was the "hero" of the *Eroica* before Napoleon was, states that the Finale had its origin "in a lowly contredanse" (Goldschmidt 1975, 30); Lewis Lockwood (Lockwood 2003, at 141) asserts (misreading KH's dates of composition for the date when the contredanses were performed) that "Beethoven also used the same material in two other works: (1) the finale [*sic*] of the Twelve Contradances (WoO 14) that he wrote for ballroom use in Vienna during *the winter of 1800-1801*" (emphasis added), and in Lockwood 1981, in the text at 459 (repr. Lockwood 1992, p. 135), and again in *id.* n. 5, he lists the contredanse as the first of four compositions making use of the theme.

Keisuke Maruyama states outright that the theme was first used in the contredanse, citing KH (Maruyama 1987, at 52); Christopher Reynolds implies without directly stating it that the "simple" contredanse came before the ballet finale (Reynolds 1982, at 49); William Kinderman thinks that Beethoven "recycled the contradance three times" (Kinderman 1995, at 80 and 89; repeated in Kinderman 2009, at 96), and Carl Dahlhaus asserts likewise (Dahlhaus [Eng. tr.] 1991, at xviii). Willy Hess finds it a wonder that any composer should discover so many riches in a piece of dance music (Hess 1962, at 30); Alexander Ringer takes TDR and Mies at their word, and assumes throughout that Beethoven composed the contredanse first, by borrowing the G-minor theme quoted in Fig. 2 above and improving it (along with its bass) (Ringer 1961). Walter Reizler assumes the "simple" contredanse came first (Reizler 1990, at 140), as does Ernst Pichler (Pichler 1994, at 197), and Frank Schneider begins his analysis with the contredanse, before taking up the ballet (Schneider 1988, at 67).

Just as Stefan Kunze relies on Deiters' argument (which he attributes to Riemann) in viewing the ballet as a subsequent improvement of the contredanse (Kunze 1972, at 132), so does Michael Heineman rely on Mies (Heineman 1992, at n. 3). Peter Schleuning and Martin Geck, while crediting the influence of the Prometheus-myth on the Symphony, nevertheless think Beethoven wrote the contredanse first, and note that its social background fit his revolutionary agenda (Schleuning and Geck 1989, at 70 and 152), as does Thomas Sipe (Sipe 1998, at 11-15), who is followed by Stephen Rumph (Rumph 2004, at 65) (referring to the ballet finale as "a recycled ballroom dance") and Katherine Syer (Syer 2006, at 179 n. 43). Not the last to join the chorus is Edmund Morris: "At first it sounded so trivial, so tum-tee-tum, that he published it in a set of party pieces for Viennese youth to dance to. No doubt he expected to forget it. But something about its rhythmic vigor stuck in his mind when he received a commission to write a ballet . . ." (Morris 2005, at 86).

The account James Hamilton-Paterson (2017) gives is ambiguous, but its plainest reading would appear to say that Beethoven wrote the contredanse first, and then reused it in the ballet: "It is a great pity that although the ballet's overture is quite often played, the rest of the music remains little known to the majority of concertgoers even though they would instantly recognize the last tune in the finale. Beethoven reused the one he had just written for the seventh of a set of twelve little contre-dances (WoO 14) . . ." (pp. 69-70). The meaning depends on how one interprets the reference in "the one he had just written" in conjunction with the verb "reused"; note that he does not mention Contredanse No. 11, also taken from the ballet finale.

Appendix G: Translation of Fishman's Study of the *Eroica* Sketches

[*Note:* The following is a translation I made and published in 1966 of the most important piece of Nathan Fishman's work: his analysis of the sketches for the Third Symphony which are contained in the Wielhorsky sketchbook (called by Fishman the "Heiligenstadt sketchbook"). This excerpt forms the last part of the first chapter of his volume of analyses - the chapter which deals with the origins and composition of the *Eroica*, whose title is "The Path to the *Eroica* Symphony (Путь к Героической Симфонии)". The translation begins with page 110 of Fishman's work and continues through the end of the chapter on page 128. Except where indicated by "[Ed.]", all footnotes are Fishman's. The only portions of the text omitted are those which deal more with Marxist philosophy than with the music being discussed.]

The first of the sketches in question is found on lines III-V on page 44. It begins with a broad cello melody reminiscent of a traditional slow introduction, similar to the introductions Beethoven used in his first two symphonies or in the overture to Die Geschöpfe des Prometheus:

This melody, which Beethoven composed just after he had completed the sketch work for the Op. 35 fugue, has much in common with the bass of the "Prometheus" theme, especially in the main turning points. At the same time Beethoven has added what is substantially new: the third of the [E-flat] harmony, which is one of the elements that serve to differentiate the beginning of the Allegro con brio from the beginning of the finale of the *Eroica*. In the sketch, however, this melody in the celli does not yet represent the main theme. We are still only in the introduction.

After the fermata other instruments, probably violins, begin to play. They repeat the first phrase of the celli in a faster tempo and then develop it in an ascending sequence that modulates from E-Flat major to F minor.

In this first stage of new harmonic movement and in the relationship between the cello and violin registers, we feel some kind of correspondence - very distant, of course - with the beginning of the Allegro con brio of the *Eroica*. Let us recall the sequence in bars 17-20 of the score that introduces a new upward direction to the basic motif of the main theme. The role that this sequence plays in the sketch we are now examining is analogous. Besides this similarity, however, our sketch has as yet nothing in common with the Allegro con brio.

After the sequence the melody of the sketch breaks off. A possibly significant segment of music is replaced by the word "etc." Beethoven then switches to the last three bars of the introduction. From the texture of music at this point, we may state with all certainty that we are dealing with an orchestral work. The chromatic melody, broken by short, specifically orchestral tremolos in the basses, leads to the tensely awaited tonic, which in turn leads to a change in meter and tempo to an Allegro in 3/4 time:

Why, these are the "four pillars"* of the "Prometheus" bass! - the reader will exclaim as he scans the first two bars of the Allegro. He is absolutely correct. Only the meter and the rhythm are different. We should listen particularly closely to alternations of length within the three-beat measures, for this is the principal rhythmic feature of the beginning of the first movement of the symphony.

After he noted down four bars of the Allegro, Beethoven once again broke off work on the sketch. Apparently he was too busy at the time to write out the theme to its end, and had to get the contour of the entire exposition down on paper in one sitting. What composition was he working on? The answer to this question remains a puzzle. The Nohl-Lenz quarrel is still unresolved. But let us not close our *Eroica* scores yet.

In our efforts to fill in some of the details a hasty Beethoven omitted, we too must also operate with short "snatches" of music. Let us forget for the time being that part of the exposition in which Beethoven states the contrasting motif of the main theme with its powerful sforzandi. Let us also forget the bridge passage in which the oboe, clarinet and flute call tenderly back and forth to one another. None of this is to be found in the sketch. Beethoven is occupied here with something else - how to approach the second subject:

---

* A designation made first by Romain Rolland [Ed.].

The lyrical melody in B-flat major, which is designated by the notation "2-da" (seconda parte) and fulfills the role of the second subject, has almost nothing in common with the exposition of the Allegro con brio. The only thing it shares with the final variant of the second subject [bars 84-94 of the score, in Fishman's analysis -Ed.] is the device of direct contrast between B-flat major and B-flat minor. On the other hand, the approach to the second theme as it stands in the sketch is very close to the bridge passage leading to the second theme in the published work. To prove this, it is enough to compare this approach with bars 63-66 of the score of the Allegro con brio where the same upward flight - to E-Flat of the third octave - occurs. These passages, performed by the first violins, could easily have originated from the broken arpeggios of dominant seventh-chords noted in the sketch.

The sketch variant of the approach to the second theme presents not only similarities with that of the published score, however, but also essential differences. For example, the use of syncopation, which is found in the sketch, also crops up in many parts of the Allegro con brio, but never in the bridge passage to the second subject. In addition, the preparation for the second theme by a tremolo in the strings is completely out of character with the completed work. (Beethoven uses a similar device for the transition from the development section to the recapitulation.) These differences, however, do not in themselves rule out the possibility of the sketch's being related to the symphony. In fact, the differences affirm the relationship; we need only consider one of the many intermediate stages that separate the 1802 sketch under consideration from the final 1804 version. Here is how the transition from the bridge passage to the second subject is stated in the second of the 1803 sketches for the exposition of the Allegro con brio:

As we see from this example, not only in 1802, but even as late as 1803, Beethoven was still planning to use both syncopation and tremolo just before the introduction of the second subject. It was only at a later stage that he gave up this intention.

Let us now turn to the second sketch of the exposition (lines X-XIV on page 44).

There is no slow introduction; the Allegro starts right off in 3/4 time. Nor does the beginning of the theme coincide as literally with the "Prometheus" bass-melody as it did in the first sketch. The theme assumes a more independent aspect. Its course is mapped out along the steps of a triad with the third falling on the weak beats. The approach to the repeat of the main theme in the upper register is quite clearly defined:

Just as in the first sketch, everything connected with the musical development, with the transition from one section of the exposition to another, comes significantly closer to the later variants than does the formulation of thematic material. It is interesting to note that although the basic motif of the main theme of the Allegro con brio is still far from being precisely determined, the variant of the motif that Beethoven uses in the concluding section has already attained full stature:

The same may be said of the tense passages for the strings in the final section of the Allegro con brio, in which the harmony changes with every eighth-note. Although it is true that these passages figure as the principal element in the bridge section and not in the concluding section, there can nevertheless be no doubt as to the accuracy of Lenz's marginal note. How can we not recognize the *Eroica* in the following excerpt?

The Allegro con brio sketches start on page 44 of the Heiligenstadt Sketchbook and continue on to page 45. In the numerous drafts on these two pages, we find many musical ideas relating both to the exposition and to the development section. Even though they are still far from the finished work, these drafts fully define the atmosphere of the symphony. Some of them Beethoven rejected, but to others he planned to return in the future, when the piece had expanded to fit the proportions in which it had been conceived, and when it had become clear exactly which details should be extracted from this "stock pile."

On the top line of page 45 we find a melody whose beginning is very similar to the sketch variant of the main theme that appears for the first time on page 44. But as early as in the second measure it takes on the rhythmical form of the final version:

Of course, this sequence was not meant to be the first bars of the exposition. It is connected either with one of the repetitions of the theme in the exposition or with the development section. And so we may state that the rhythmic design that makes up the basic motif first crystallized with the formulation of one of the developmental stages of the theme rather than with that of the beginning of the Allegro con brio.

From the preceding examples of the original formulation of the material of the first movement of the *Eroica*, we can see that the argument between Lenz and Nohl was not only the result but also the cause of many misconceptions. Since Lenz left his "Eroica" indication (on page 44 of the Heiligenstadt Sketchbook) unexplained by not substantiating it with publication of the sketches and allowing it to be torn apart by Nohl, Beethoveniana has not paid it much attention or even treated it seriously. The first of the variants of the exposition of the Allegro con brio, written in the 1803 sketchbook, has been unanimously accepted as the first variant of any part of the exposition. But in fact, on the basis of the creative process we must propose a different starting point, which is opposed not only to Bekker's views, but also to those of Nottebohm, Rolland and many others. The second theme of the bridge passage, with its stormy headlong and impetuous movement, was written much earlier than the tender melody of the lyrical first theme of the bridge passage, and the formulation of the concluding section preceded the crystallization of the beginning of the exposition.* As for the basic motif of the main theme, we see from the Heiligenstadt Sketchbook that it originates from rather long and complicated transmutations of the "Prometheus" bass. The opinion [Paul Bekker's - *cf.* n. 15 in ch. 1, at p. 3 - Ed.] that Beethoven could have borrowed this theme from Mozart is thus refuted. It also becomes clear that the exact formulation of the theme in this instance was not a requisite but to a great extent a result of the musical conception of the whole.

The complex process by which the second and the "new" [this is Fishman's appellation for the E-minor theme of the development -Ed.] themes of the Allegro con brio took shape - as reflected in the Heiligenstadt Sketchbook - also affords much material for observation. In both the first and the second variants of the exposition written on page 44, the second theme does not resemble its final version. This should not surprise us, because later sketches published by G. Nottebohm show that Beethoven did not complete the second subject in its final form until he had reached the very last stages of composing the entire symphony.

The second of the variants of the second subject written on page 44 displays an important peculiarity which may most profitably be evaluated by comparison not with its final version but once again with an intermediate stage. This variant, composed in 1802, should be contrasted with an 1803 sketch of the "new" (and not the secondary) theme of the Allegro con brio:

As we see from this comparison, the theme that served as the basis for the later formulation of the "new" theme of the development originally played the role of the secondary theme of the exposition. But even after he had finished this "new" theme, the composer still did not incorporate it into the development section, but was planning to allot it the place in the exposition that belongs to the second subject.

---

* It is worthy of note that elements of the concluding section of the Allegro con brio are more distinctly defined in the 1802 sketch than in the early 1803 sketches. And in the last (fourth) sketch made in 1803, it seems as if Beethoven is returning to the variant he composed a year earlier.

Does this mean that when Beethoven began work on the Allegro con brio of the *Eroica* he had no idea at all that he would include the "new" theme in the development section? Let us turn to a sketch of the development section on the second line of page 45. In the first bars of this line we find octave jumps that obviously represent the climax of some contemplated upward movement. A lyrical theme follows the jumps and is in turn followed by the transition to the recapitulation (on lines III-IV). This lyrical theme does not have much in common with the sketches of the exposition. But does this really new (third) theme bear any resemblance to the "new" theme in the development section of the Allegro con brio? No, it does not. But what if we compare it, as we have done before, to an intermediate stage instead of to the completed composition? Suppose we contrast this 1802 variant with an 1803 sketch for the second subject - and not the "new" theme:

It seems that in the process of the sketch work (which lasted for two years), the second subject of the exposition and the "new" theme of the development changed places. Moreover, once we turn from the Heiligenstadt Sketchbook and concentrate on the 1803 sketches for the Allegro con brio, we will also discover that in the process of its formulation the second subject was influenced to a certain degree by the earlier formulation of the "new" theme. Here, for example, is a variant of the "new" theme as it appears in the first of the 1803 sketches for the development section (even at this point, the variant is close to the final version):

And here is one of the last sketch variants of the second subject:

112

Эскиз 1803 г.

NB

The general idea of the process is as follows: the first variant of the second subject of the exposition, i.e., the variant that created the "new" theme of the development, is completely dissolved in this "new" theme. Once the "new" theme takes shape, it pays back the theme of the second subject in kind. The result is a peculiar type of bifurcation: one variant of the second subject is used for the development section, and another for the exposition. This explanation will clear up the puzzlement which George Grove felt when he wrote: "Oddly enough, Beethoven made very little use of this [secondary] theme. In the development section he does not return to it at all, and it is not until the recapitulation that it again turns up in its proper place."*

If Grove had seen the Heiligenstadt Sketchbook, he would have realized that the secondary theme of the exposition and the "new" theme of the development section are completely inseparable from each other, and that the lyrical episode of the development section is really the musical development of the secondary part of the first movement (and here we mean the secondary part in its broadest sense).

But why in the process of his sketch work did Beethoven feel it necessary to switch the places of the secondary and "new" themes - both of which are merely variants of the secondary part of the first movement, again in the broad sense? The reason is probably that as the heroic image grew, the usual exposition framework of the second subject became too limited for the embodiment of a melody that was to express the highest of ideals. A series of preparatory musical and dramatic events were needed. This is why Beethoven transferred the "Prometheus" Urmelodie from the exposition to the development section. This may also be one of the reasons for the colossal proportions of the development section: it surpasses all other Beethoven development sections in absolute and relative size.†

---

* G. Grove, Beethoven und seine neun Symphonien (London, 1906), p. 62.
† The table below gives the lengths for the expositions and development sections of all nine Beethoven symphonies (this table is based on calculations made by A. Lorenz in his Neues Beethoven-Jahrbuch in 1924):

After the first draft of the new theme which we saw on line 2, page 45 of the Heiligenstadt Sketchbook, Beethoven made another short draft, as we have already noted, that treats the moment of transition from the development section to the recapitulation. Our examination of this draft, however, should be prefaced by a well-known and very humorous anecdote from Beethoven's life.

It would be hard to find in all of musical literature a two-bar phrase that gave rise to so much idle talk as the cue for the second horn before the recapitulation of the Allegro con brio of the Third Symphony (bars 398-399 of the score). F. Ries, who was present at the rehearsal of the first performance of the symphony, thought when he heard it that the horn player had come in too early. "The damned horn player can't even count," Ries exclaimed. Beethoven was furious at his student. "I believe," Ries continues, "I was not far from getting a slap in the face."*

Ries, however, was by far not the only one to doubt the accuracy of the horn's entrance. Several nineteenth century Italian conductors considered it as a misprint at the end of the development section and made the horn-player play his entrance in the tenor clef, i.e., in

Sym. No.	No. of bars		Ratio of the length of	
	Exp.	Devel.	Exposition	: Development
1	97	68	1.4	: 1
2	100	84	1.2	: 1
3	147	250	1.0	: 1.7
4	154	152	1.0	: 1
5	124	123	1.0	: 1
6	138	140	1.0	: 1
7	114	97	1.2	: 1
8	103	86	1.2	: 1
9	159	141	1.1	: 1

* Biographische notizen über Ludwig van Beethoven, p. 94.

B-Flat major.* Even Wagner was misled on this point: although he left the horn part untouched, he asked the second violins to tremolo during these two bars on the third (G) and not the seventh of the dominant -- A-Flat.† Berlioz, too, considered this famous "Cumulus" an oddity. "Strictly speaking," he writes, "it is difficult to find serious justification for this musical caprice. If Beethoven really did stand by this device, and if the anecdotes based on it contain a grain of truth, I must confess it was an awkward caprice."‡

Nottebohm has refuted these doubts by establishing that the paradoxical harmony in bars 398-399 of the score of the *Eroica* is not the result of an accident but rather of long and careful consideration on the part of Beethoven before he included it in the final copy of the score. Nottebohm demonstrated that in the 1803 sketches there are variants with an even sharper harmony: the strings tremolo on the third of the dominant (D) and not the seventh, thereby setting up a minor second against the tonic:§

This draft was made on page 30 of the 1803 sketchbook. In the same book, however, we find other variants of the transition to the recapitulation in which the composer is obviously unsure as to the advisability of using such an effect. For example, a variant of the transition found on page 33 is almost identical to the final variant, whereas a later variant, found on page 35, has no trace whatsoever of the pre-recapitulation entrance of the horn:

---

* G. Grove, Beethoven und seine neun Symphonien (London, 1906), p. 66.

† *Ibid.*

‡ Г. Берлиоз [H. Berlioz]. Симфонии Бетховена. [The Symphonies of Beethoven.] (St. Petersburg: 1896), p. 16. (A travers chants, p. 22.)

§ *Cf.* N1880 [Mies (ed.) 1924], at 29.

Let us now compare these variations with the draft of the transition to the recapitulation which was composed a year earlier and is to be found on the third and fourth lines of page 45 of the Heiligenstadt Sketchbook:

The solo horn does not yet have the entrance that caused Beethoven to get so angry with Ries. But the combination tonic under dominant is very clearly outlined. Thus, the "false" entrance that has caused such a fuss among conductors and horn-players has behind it the careful consideration which we have already studied. And it cannot be overemphasized that Beethoven was concerned about the moment of the transition to the recapitulation at the very first stage of his work on the symphony. This shows the great importance Beethoven attached to this point in the musical drama, a point connected with the affirmation of victory. It is no coincidence that after the sketch for the transition to the recapitulation, we find a whole series of drafts (lines V-IX on page 45 of the Heiligenstadt Sketchbook) based on a joyful fanfare of victory:

116

These fanfares appear in the *Eroica,* but not in the Allegro con brio. We will be returning to the above example somewhat later when we talk about the marvelous metamorphosis of the Minuetto serioso into a "hunting" scherzo. And now let us examine the creative processes behind the second movement of the symphony -- the brilliant Marcia funebre. It would be difficult to name another period in history when Trauermusik played such an important role in social life as the years preceding Beethoven's activity as a composer of symphonies. The French revolution invoked the patriotic Muse to strew heroes' graves with flowers. M. J. Chenier addressed composers directly: "Somber, touching harmonies, let us hear your chords!"*

Francois Gossec's Marche lugubre, first performed at Mirabeau's funeral, enjoyed immense popularity and became the model for many marches funebres composed in the nineteenth century. The line of succession leads straight to Beethoven, and it may even be said that to a certain extent Gossec anticipated Beethoven's Trauermusik. As an example let us compare the middle section of Gossec's Marche lugubre with the first sketches for the Marcia funebre sulla morte d'un eroe from the A-Flat Major Sonata, Op 26., Of course the similarity is caused in this case by the common element of a tragic experience and by the unity of the musical and inspirational base. This unity, however, is in itself significant.†

---

* *Cf.* Ж. Тьерсо. Песни и празднества французской революции ["Songs and Festivals of the French Revolution"]. Moscow, 1933, p. 52.
† Gossec's march is cited from the book Сжатый очерк истории музыки ["Short Sketches in the History of Music"], Е. М. Браудо [E. M. Braudo] (Moscow, 1935), p.159. The sketch for Beethoven's march appears on page 56 of the Landsberg sketchbook, which contains sketches for the ballet Die Geschöpfe des Prometheus, as discussed earlier.

But if Gossec's funeral march is a separate work destined for performance by a military band, Beethoven solves the problem of how to integrate this type of revolutionary music into a symphonic sonata cycle. For proof of how effective his solution was, we do not need to confine ourselves to Beethoven's work. We know, for example, that Beethoven's combination of a funeral march and a Moto perpetuo in his Sonata Op. 26 was later richly developed in Chopin's B Minor Sonata. Of course we must not conclude that Chopin's brilliant monophonic writing should be examined through the prism of the finale of Beethoven's Sonata in A-Flat Major. The content of these works is basically different. But the dramatic principles reflect a direct relationship.*

In fact, a sort of Moto perpetuo follows the funeral march in the *Eroica* too. The conception here is basically the same as in the Op. 26 Sonata: a man's death is transitory, while mankind lives into eternity. But in the Symphony, the Moto perpetuo (Scherzo) does not end the work. It is merely the transition to the final apotheosis - the image of a nation-wide celebration which we might describe in the words of Peyan:

"This music, these cries of joy flying upward to the heavens, these waves of a fraternal people, waves whose swelling - great and small - expressed both a burst of grateful ecstasy and serene tranquility of social conscience . . . and finally the hymn of victory,

---

* A detailed analysis of the question of the derived connections between Beethoven's A-Flat Major Sonata and Chopin's B-Minor Sonata will be found in the collection published by the Beethoven Centennial in Vienna in 1927: Beethoven-Zentenarfeier. Internationaler Musikhistorischer Kongress ("Chopins Sonaten und ihr Verhältnis zum Beethovenschen Stil," pp. 138-141).

uniting the people with their representatives, hands raised, stretched toward the heavens, taking oaths before the sun . . ." *

Connected by the Moto perpetuo with the apotheosis-celebration, the funeral march of the *Eroica* also directly anticipates the Allegro con brio - the tragic canvas of the battle. If the finale displays a hitherto unknown grandiosity in the development of the variation form, the first movement does the same for the sonata-allegro form. We may ask whether the funeral march, standing between these two giants, could have held its own if it had been written in the tripartite form which we usually associate with this type of music, i.e., in the form of Gossec's Marche lugubre, the Marcia funebre sulla morte d'un eroe in Beethoven's Sonata Op. 26, or the funeral march from Chopin's B-Minor Sonata? Scarcely. The construction of the *Eroica*'s funeral march had to be integrated with that of the first and last movements. And in fact it is just as much the model of the symphonizing of a march as the finale is of the symphonizing of the variation form. It also boasts of a development section in which Beethoven makes wide use of polyphonic development techniques. "Three sources are united in this magnificent picture," writes I. J. Ryzhkin, "the funeral marches of the French Revolution, the tragic pages of polyphonic art (J. S. Bach) and the slow movements of the classical symphony - images of social and national significance, profound philosophical thoughts, and individual psychological character."†

One more source must be added to these three. It is found outside the purely musical plane and is characteristic not only of Beethoven's Marcia funebre but of all burial ceremonies in revolutionary France at the end of the 18th century . . .

[There follows a passage describing the Greek and Roman traditions employed in these ceremonies, which is omitted from this translation. -Ed.]

. . . All this and much more is reminiscent of scenes like the one that inspired Berlioz as he conducted the funeral march of the *Eroica* - the burial of Palant in the 11th book of Virgil's Aeneid.‡ Of course Berlioz's parallel is not based on any factual data and must not be

---

* From the report and decree of June 29, 1794, of the Committee on General Education. The quoted excerpt appears in the account of the Revolutionary Festival of February 20, which is given in Romain Rolland's book The National Theater, pp. 114-115 of the Russian edition published in 1932.

† И. Я. Рыжкин. Бетховен и классический симфонизм [I. J. Rizhkin, Beethoven and Classical Symphonism] (Moscow 1938), p. 11.

‡ Berlioz cites the following lines in his analysis of the funeral march (*see* "A travers

119

taken literally. He does not suggest that Beethoven actually had Virgil's classical description of a funeral before his eyes as he composed the funeral march. But profound artist that he was, Berlioz guessed the presence of a link between Beethoven's march and the tragic heroes of antiquity. A century after Berlioz musicology is beginning to understand this link and to apply it in its studies. It is no coincidence that J. Racek hears the embodiment of scenes from Aeschylus in this march.* When he composed his funeral march - "in honor of the memory of a great man" - Beethoven, as well as others of his fellow revolutionaries, was invoking the spirits of the past and conjuring up the dead for the exaltation of a new battle. Let us recall here the passages he copied into his diary out of Homer. And let us recall his dictum: "No matter what people say about the past, it still appears as the present."†

The main theme of the *Eroica*'s funeral march is one of the greatest revelations of music as an art and at the same time one of the most popular of all musical motifs. Words cannot describe the depth of the impression it makes on all who hear it. It is not that its emotional meaning is unclear - rather, it is precisely the opposite: it is much clearer than words. It is expressed in music with the utmost degree of clarity, a clarity that words cannot attain when it comes to the universal expression of the condition of the soul and character of man's experiences.

What can we say, for example, about the melody with the sharply dotted rhythm in the third bar of the Marcia? Anyone who still has an ounce of feeling left in him cannot fail to feel compassion when he hears it. Many are reminded of those sacred minutes before the final departure of a loved one. Who can describe these last moments in words?

Beethoven too had a hard time choosing the necessary "words." It is clear from the sketches that every turn of the main theme of the March was literally the object of a stubborn struggle; he was searching for this funereal melody, later to become immortal, in the inmost recesses of his heart. How did he find it? How was it written?

---

chants," p. 22):
  Chariots stained with blood carry the Rutuls
  Next walks the war horse Eton without any medals
  Crying, with large tears rolling down his cheeks.
* Beethoven (Praha [Prague] 1956), p.84.
† Cited in A. Leitzmann, Beethovens Briefe und persönliche Aufzeichnungen, p. 62.

The reader is already aware that in 1800, while he was working on the ninth number of the ballet Die Geschöpfe des Prometheus, Beethoven conceived a tragic motif to express the sufferings and death of Prometheus that later was directly incorporated into the symphony. [*See* Chapter 3 ("The Music of the Ballet") in the main text. -Ed.] But at that time the idea was only "understood" (Beethoven's word) and not yet fully "felt." The sketch designated "Prometheus weint" is not used in the ballet.

Later, in 1802, Beethoven composed the Marcia in C minor for the fifth variation of Op. 34. Here one finds motifs outlined which are close to the opening phrases of the *Eroica* funeral march. On the whole, however, the fifth variation from Op. 34 cannot at all measure up to the Adagio assai of the symphony.

Finally, the composer seems to find a rapprochement between the burial motif of Op. 34 and the unrealized sketch for the ballet. This rapprochement forms the base on which the main theme of the funeral march of the symphony was later to grow:*

Thus, if the main theme of the Allegro con brio originates from a fusion of the Prometheus melody and the Prometheus bass, the main theme of the Marcia funebre is an integral of a different type: not a fusion but rather a coupling of the C minor Op. 34 variation and the Prometheus weint sketch. If we take the entire *Eroica* as a unified, inseparable whole, two main themes come to the fore and reign over all others. The first of these themes is the Prometheus theme which comes from the ballet by way of Op. 35, and undergoes manifold modifications in the Allegro con brio, the finale and, as I will demonstrate below, in the Scherzo. The second theme dominates in the Marcia funebre and does not undergo any basic modification in the process of development.

---

* I have reproduced here only the upper voice of the Marcia sketch [for op. 34] made on page 16 of the Heiligenstadt Sketchbook.

From the above example (Illustration 72) to the final version of the main theme of the Funeral March there was still a long way to go. In Nottebohm's publication of the 1803 sketchbook there are only several drafts of the March, cited in the sequence in which they appear on pages 6, 42, 43 and 49 of this book. But in all probability Nottebohm did not take full account of the chronological order of the sketches. In particular, he did not pay any attention to the fact that the sketch on page 42 was most likely written not before, but after the original variant of the sketch on page 43. This fact is of great significance for characterizing formulation of the theme:

The first sketch we find on page 6 is stated not in 2/4 but in 4/4 -- twice as long as the final version. The decision that followed shortly after to change the meter was probably prompted by a desire to emphasize the quick forward motion of the music. Perhaps the inconsistency between the metronome marking (an eighth-note = 80) and the tempo marking (Adagio assai) that has been noted by F. Weingartner* may also be traced to the same source: a slow tempo, incompatible with the static character he was looking for, seemed to Beethoven a greater evil than the tendency to liven up the movement.

Also reflected in these first sketches is the process by which Beethoven experimented with various theme-climax points. Even when he was composing the ninth number for the ballet *Die Geschöpfe des Prometheus* in 1800, Beethoven knew that the highest note should fall on the sixth of the scale and would be preceded by an interval of a diminished fifth. But both in the 1800 and the first 1803 sketch, this high point falls on the weak beat of the sixth measure of the theme, i.e., at the end of the phrase's climax. It was not until later that he found that point which best dominates over the entire orchestra. This point, of course, turned out to be the first beat of the sixth measure. To make this point stand out more clearly, Beethoven prepared it by means of tense, upward movement (this is connected with filling in the diminished fifth with notes of the C minor scale).

Determining a place for the climax and an approach to the climax did not yet complete the theme. The last two bars of the phrase - the post-climactic descending line - still had to be written. Beethoven vacillates between allotting the entire bar, 3/4, 1/2 or 1/4 of the bar to the melody's peak; he tries to descend by using a sharp, dotted rhythm and a broad wave-like line. He is also unsure how he will place the final periods, whether he will bring the theme to a stop on the first beat of the last bar or to a softened, weak and feminine ending. The guideposts that direct him to his final decision are graphically demonstrated by the corrections he makes in the fourth sketch: everything that could for any reason be associated with pitiful sentimentality he got rid of. Beethoven concluded the theme with the masculine motif:

---

* Ratschläge für Aufführungen der Symphonien Beethovens (Leipzig, 1916), pp. 43-4.

Although its genesis is not connected with the Prometheus Urmelodie, the symphony's funeral march is not free from functional correlations with various of the Urmelodie's modifications. The relationship between the two is especially strong in the second (E-flat major) theme of the funeral march when -- according to A. Al'švang's successful description - "a stream of heroic emotions break through the cloud of the funeral genre bearing the news that the heroic idea lives on even after the hero perishes":*

The character of this parallel differs essentially from those drawn above between the Prometheus theme and the main theme of the Allegro con brio. In the first movement the common ground of these themes consists of the Prometheus bass that Beethoven uses as a point of departure in both cases. And even though the themes move further and further apart as Beethoven works and reworks them, they still retain their inner unity. Here, in the funeral march, we observe the reverse. The basic theme has nothing in common with the Prometheus theme. But as the symphony develops as a whole, Beethoven finds ways of bringing the new and the old themes closer together and gradually unifying them.

The use of this creative principle exceeds the limits of the formation of musical themes as such and belongs rather to the area of development. It is interesting to contrast the funeral march's brilliant fugato with the *Eroica*-fugue of the finale from this viewpoint. If we ignore the basic difference of concrete music content, we will uncover certain methodological similarities in the construction of the form. Thus, for example, in both the Marcia and in the finale polyphony is used as a powerful means of broadening the framework of an originally unpolyphonic form (in one case variation and in the other tripartite); both the finale's fugue and the march have as their starting points an inverted theme; in both cases the polyphonic foreground unfolds against a backdrop of longer notes. Moreover, the Marcia fugato represents the peak of sorrow - one of the most tragic passages in all music literature, whereas the *Eroica*-fugue of the finale is a paean of joy and one of the most optimistic passages in all music literature.

---

* А. Альшванг. Бетховен [A. Al'švang, Beethoven (Moscow, 1952)], p. 139.

Analyzing the sketches of the first movement of the symphony in the Heiligenstadt Sketchbook, we met with a misunderstanding arising from a misinterpretation of Lenz's indication "Eroica" on page 44. A similar type of indication -- in the upper right-hand corner of page 16 next to Beethoven's note "Todtenmarsch" - has led to a completely different type of misunderstanding.

Beethoven's note refers here to two notes which are the upbeat to the fifth variation of Op. 34. Once he had outlined these notes and defined them with the word "Todtenmarsch," Beethoven designated the next segment of the variation - which he did not write out - with the word "etc.", and going on to the next page, wrote the ending of the fifth and the beginning of the sixth variation of the F major cycle.

But when Lenz was looking through the Heiligenstadt Sketchbook in the Wielhorsky library, he was so much taken by the word "Todtenmarsch" that he did not think to examine its environment and so considered these two notes the opening of the funeral march of the Third Symphony and wrote "Eroica" next to them. This inaccuracy is strongly reflected in Lenz's Catalog,* from whence it became accepted by musicologists. It has since led to much distortion of the facts of the history of the composition of the Third Symphony.†

Thus, for example, A. Thayer, who proposed that the Op. 85 oratorio dates from 1801,‡ related the sketch of the funeral march mentioned by Lenz with the reminiscences of a contemporary of Beethoven - a certain Doctor Bertolini - who states that Beethoven composed the funeral march for the death of General Abercrombie who fell in action on March 28, 1801 with General Menu's troops in Egypt. This would seem to be confirmed by Beethoven's sketch of 1801 that is supposedly related to the funeral march.

However, since Lenz says nothing in his Catalog about the presence of sketches relating to the Allegro con brio and the Scherzo in the sketchbook from the Wielhorsky library; and since Nottebohm wrote in 1880 that Beethoven did not start work on the symphony

---

* With these two notes in mind, Lenz writes in his Catalog about a "hint" of the *Eroica*'s funeral march in Wielhorsky's sketchbook without connecting this "hint" with Op. 34. (*See* Lenz, Vol. III, p. 222.)

† Although L. Nohl pointed out this inaccuracy in his polemic with Lenz, it was somehow just this point that has escaped later critics' attention. (*See* Nohl, p. 97).

‡ *See* Thayer, Vol. II, p. 421. I will be giving more detailed information about the dating of the Op. 85 oratorio on pp. 170-171 of this study.

before 1802, scholars accepted the opinion - and accepted it as indisputable - that plans for the even (second and fourth) and odd (first and third) movements of the symphony are separated by a two-year period; that the funeral march was inserted as a supplement for some kind of special reason, etc., etc. Even in the most detailed recent scholarly indices of Beethoven's work (including Kinsky's index) we cannot find a precise dating of the *Eroica*.

Although he connects the short Todtenmarsch fragment (which in reality belongs to Op. 34) with the symphony, Lenz does not mention in his Catalog the sketches from lines VI-IX on page 44 of the Heiligenstadt Sketchbook. The fact that these drafts are surrounded by sketches for the Allegro con brio of the *Eroica*, however, cannot but evoke the following question: are not they too related to the same Symphony?

The first of these drafts bears the title Adagio in C major. The theme of this Adagio, which lasts for four bars on line VI, has certain traits in common with the oboe melody at the beginning of the Maggiore from the Adagio assai of the Symphony (bars 69-70 of the second movement). True, the sketch is in 6/8 and the Maggiore of the funeral march is in 2/4. But then again, the Maggiore theme in the symphony is backed up by almost continuous triplets.

After the Adagio theme, i.e., after the "etc." note, we find two excerpts on lines VI-VIII, p. 44, in which this triplet background is represented. In the fourth measure of line VII Beethoven breaks off his statement of this background to note down a broad, deeply mournful melody to be played by the bassoon:

Next comes the last of the excerpts relating to the C major Adagio. It is a line that undergoes much intensification and is accompanied by the dynamic marking: "cres. più forte e sempre più voce" which gives way to a quick abatement of intensity. The marking "cresc. sempre più forte" also figures with the same significance before the Maggiore in the Marcia.

All these data, of course, do not permit us to state that lines VI-VIII on page 44 make up the first draft of the Maggiore from the funeral march. But let us turn to two other markings which Beethoven made at the end of line VIII and the beginning of line IX. The first of them runs: "aus dem Adagio im M." The second is "Minuetto serioso" (the title of the sketch on line IX). What can "M." mean? There are two possible answers: "M." stands for either the Marcia or the Minuetto which were to follow the Adagio. If we opt for Marcia, then there is no need to continue arguing whether the Adagio in C major belongs to the symphony or not (let us keep in mind that the Adagio is in the same "environment" as sketches for the first movement of the *Eroica*). But can we come to the same conclusion if the "M." stands for Minuetto and not Marcia?

Let us turn to the sketches for the Minuetto serioso and trace the development of its theme. Here is the original variant:

And here is the development and final variant:

Although the last of these sketch-variants, which comes from the Heiligenstadt Sketchbook, is close, as we see, to the final version of the Scherzo of the Third Symphony, it is also separated from it by a two-year period. And from the sketches published by Nottebohm we know that Beethoven did not make the decision to turn the third

127

movement of the *Eroica* from a minuet into a scherzo until he had reached page 60 of the 1803 sketchbook, i.e., not long after he had completely finished work on the symphony. This "jump" from a minuet to a scherzo in 1803 (I have used here Nottebohm's expression "Sprunge"*) is graphically described by Rolland:

". . . We have a striking example in the third movement of the *Eroica*, which he began as a minuet and continued as a minuet until the trio (trio in its generally accepted form) and even further. Then, suddenly returning to the minuet, he sketched the following:

His pen begins to twitch. He writes 'Presto.' Down with the measured grace of the minuet! Up with a brilliant, bubbling Scherzo!"†

Although both Nottebohm and Rolland mention this turning point on page 60 of the 1803 sketches, neither of them points out that the reason for the final metamorphosis is the distinctive meeting of the minuet with the main theme of the Allegro con brio. Here is how the 1803 sketch of the Trio looks up to the point where it stops being a minuet:

Trio

This is the point where Beethoven's "pen began to twitch." Beethoven no longer returned to the Minuet. But let us compare this Trio with the main theme of the Allegro con brio:

It is obvious that the "jump" was directly connected with the recurrent modification of the Prometheus theme. Further on this theme continues to gain strength, not only in the Trio where it represents the "hunters' music" but also in the Moto perpetuo:

---

* N1880 [Mies (ed.) 1924], at 46.
† Rolland, p. 93.

As we can see, it is again the Prometheus theme - the symphony's Urmelodie - that plays a decisive role: this time in turning the third movement from a minuet into a scherzo. Now there can no longer be any doubt about the fact that the Adagio in C major is a draft of the middle of the second movement and that the indication "aus dem Adagio im M." refers to the implied recapitulation of this movement.

* * * * *

The data we have gathered from our analysis permit us to make the following conclusions concerning the history of the composition of the *Eroica* Symphony.

The first musical idea of the funeral march arose in Beethoven's creative imagination as early as 1800 while he was working on *Die Geschöpfe des Prometheus,* and is directly related to the reproduction in music of the sufferings and death of Prometheus. It may also be at this time that Beethoven made his decision to compose a symphonic work that would include Trauermusik.

The Variations Op. 34 as well as those of the Op. 35 cycle may be looked upon as a preparatory stage to the composition of the symphony. And we may consider the sketches for the fifth variation (Todtenmarsch) of Op. 34 and sketches for the introduction, fugues and a number of variations of Op. 35 as the first drafts of the second and fourth movements of the *Eroica*.

The theory generally accepted among Beethoven scholars, that the second and fourth movements were written in 1801 and the first and third in 1803 is absolutely false. The fact is that Beethoven started work on all the movements almost simultaneously in the summer of 1802 when he was in Heiligenstadt.

The finale of the *Eroica* is closely related not only to the final number but also to the introduction and first number of *Die Geschöpfe des Prometheus* both by its thematic unity with them and the similarity of expressive devices Beethoven used in both instances.

The composition of the first part of the symphony grew directly out of work on the *Eroica*-fugue. The main theme of the first movement, as well as a number of other themes used in the symphony, are modifications of the Prometheus theme.

After considering the data presented here, we may accept as fully established the fact that Prometheus' heroic image is relevant not only to the fourth but to all the movements of the symphony. Beethoven himself apparently felt no reason to hide this, for in 1803 when he was doing his most intensive work on the symphony, he insisted on publishing the Op. 35 Prometheus cycle.

Beethoven's interpretation of the ancient myth, however, turned out to differ essentially from that of Viganò in his scenario for *Die Geschöpfe des Prometheus*.

As we know, of Aeschylus' famous Prometheus trilogy, only the tragedy *Prometheus Bound* and fragments of the following tragedy *Prometheus Unchained* have been preserved. And because we have no remnants of the drama *Prometheus the Fire-Bearer* we cannot establish the position it occupied within the cycle. The question of whether it was to be the opening or closing part has remained unresolved by literary scholars.

Certain literary historians cite the mythological variant that has Hercules liberate Prometheus according to the will of Zeus and have often tried to prove that it was Aeschylus' intention to censure Prometheus' "revolt." Such an interpretation, which grossly contradicts the content of *Prometheus Bound*, has been strongly protested by progressive artists. Here is what Shelley had to say about this in the Introduction to his lyrical drama *Prometheus Unbound*.

"But, in truth, I was averse to a catastrophe so feeble as that of reconciling the Champion with the Oppressor of Mankind. The moral interest of the fable, which is so powerfully sustained by the sufferings and endurance of Prometheus, would be annihilated if we could conceive of him as unsaying his high language and quailing before his successful and perfidious adversary."*

Judging by its scenario, *Die Geschöpfe des Prometheus* had very little in common with Greek drama. Thus, for example, the unchaining (rebirth) of Prometheus is accomplished in the ballet by a nature god (Pan) and not by a human (Hercules). As far as the general

---

* P. Shelley, Complete Works [in Russian - St. Petersburg, 1904], vol. II, p. 334.

outline of the ballet is concerned, we have the following: first Prometheus the Fire-Bearer, then Prometheus Bound, and finally Prometheus Unchained.

We must also emphasize in this connection that in the second part of this outline, Prometheus is not only temporarily defeated, but killed (Melpomene kills him in the ninth number, and Pan resurrects him in the tenth). This is why we find the indication "Prometheus mort" several times in the 1800 sketchbook.

As he composed the music to the ballet, Beethoven could alter nothing of Viganò's outline except to include a symphonic overture depicting the image of Prometheus the theomachist. But in the Symphony, after having painted the battle for the bright ideal of mankind in the first movement, the composer seems to reconstruct the outline of what is to come: the death of Prometheus - the second movement, the rebirth (liberation) of Prometheus - the third movement, and finally, Prometheus the Fire-Bearer - the fourth movement. If in the second movement Beethoven expressed deep sorrow for the sacrifice in the name of justice, in the third movement as he composed the hunter's music perhaps he saw before him an archer who never misses aiming his arrows at Zeus's cruel eagle. And the fourth movement is the general celebration, whose apotheosis is to be found in the hymn of glory, a loving song of peace.

In 1802, the same year in which Beethoven started work on the *Eroica*, Herder's *Prometheus Unchained* appeared for the first time. Prometheus' words to the Ocean could have served as an epigraph to Beethoven's Symphony:

"The distance of world space is invisible, And all that is in it belongs to everyone."*

But why, the reader will ask, did Bonaparte's name originally figure on the title page of the Symphony?

Let us recall Lenin's definition of Napoleon's historical role . . .

The idea of writing a composition to glorify Napoleon Bonaparte came to Beethoven when Napoleon was still consul and perhaps only general of the French revolutionary army. There is nothing surprising in the fact that Beethoven should associate the image of Napoleon with that of Prometheus as a herald of ideas of progress. Moreover, Beethoven never in the least aimed at "depicting" Napoleon himself. If he had, the inclusion of a

---

* J. Herder, Sämtliche Werke (Tübingen, 1806), Vol. VI, p. 73.

funeral march would have been completely nonsensical; Napoleon was on the march from one victorious battle to the next.

But at the same time the presence of a funeral march in the Symphony was also a reason for Beethoven's adding "in honor of the memory of a great man" to the title page after Napoleon's coronation. This addition was made not without sarcasm. It reflects a change in Beethoven's attitude towards Napoleon, who had changed from the herald of freedom into its stifler, from the champion of mankind into its oppressor.

Appendix H: Beethoven's Heiligenstadt Testament

[The following is the text and a translation of a four-page document found among Beethoven's papers after his death, and first published to the world in October 1827. By its own testimony, Beethoven wrote and signed it while he was staying at Heiligenstadt, in October 1802. He addressed it to his two brothers Carl and (Nikolaus) Johann, although in the three places where the latter's name should stand, it has been rubbed out, for unknown reasons. (Some have speculated that after his younger brother came to Vienna in 1795, and expressed his desire to drop his given name "Nikolaus" and be known by the name of their father [Johann van Beethoven, an alcoholic and cruel parent whom Beethoven loathed], Ludwig did not acquiesce – and was so opposed to it that he could not bring himself, during his emotional turmoil at Heiligenstadt, to address his younger brother by that name.) Since it disposes of his money and property to them, it has been given the title "Testament," although Beethoven replaced it with another will before he died. Maynard Solomon (1998) observes that the original appears to be a "fair copy" that replaced an earlier and perhaps more histrionic draft; even so, its emotion still resonates.]

[First page of the autograph]

{An} für meine Brüder *Carl* und   Beethowen

O ihr Menschen die ihr mich für Feindseelig störisch oder Misantropisch haltet oder erkläret, wie unrecht thut ihr mir, ihr wißt nicht die geheime ursache von dem, was euch so scheinet, mein Herz und mein Sinn waren von Kindheit an für das zarte Gefühl des Wohlwollens, selbst große Handlungen zu verrichten dazu war ich immer aufgelegt, aber bedenket nur daß seit 6 Jahren ein heilloser Zustand mich befallen, durch unvernünftige Ärzte verschlimmert, von Jahr zu Jahr in der Hofnung gebessert zu werden, betrogen, endlich zu dem überblick eines **daurenden Übels** das (dessen Heilung vieleicht Jahre dauren oder gar unmöglich ist) gezwungen, mit einem feurigen Lebhaften Temperamente gebohren selbst empfänglich für die Zerstreuungen der Gesellschaft, muste ich früh mich absondern, einsam mein Leben zubringen, wollte ich auch zuweilen mich einmal über alles das hinaussezen, o wie hart wurde ich dur[ch] die verdoppelte traurige Erfahrung meines schlechten Gehör's dann zurückgestoßen, und doch war's mir noch nicht möglich den Menschen zu sagen: sprecht lauter, schreyt, denn ich bin Taub, ach wie wär es möglich daß ich da die Schwäche **eines Sinnes** angeben sollte, der bey mir in einem Vollkommenern Grade als bey andern seyn sollte, einen Sinn denn ich einst in der grösten Vollkommenheit besaß, in einer Vollkommenheit, wie ihn wenige von meinem Fache gewiß haben noch gehabt haben – o ich kann es nicht, drum verzeiht, wenn ihr mich da zurückweichen sehen werdet, wo ich mich gerne unter euch mischte, doppelt Wehe thut mir mein unglück, indem ich dabey verkannt werden muß, für mich darf Erholung in Menschlicher Gesellschaft, feinere unterredungen, Wechselseitige Ergießungen nicht statt haben, ganz allein fast nur so viel als es die höchste Nothwendigkeit fodert, darf ich mich in Gesellschaft einlassen, wie ein Verbannter muß ich leben, nahe ich mich einer Gesellschaft, so überfällt mich eine heiße Ängstlichkeit, indem ich befürchte in Gefahr gesezt zu werden, meine[n] Zustand merken zu laßen – so war es denn auch dieses halbe Jahr, was ich auf dem Lande zubrachte, von meinem Vernünftigen Arzte aufgefodert, so viel als möglich mein Gehör zu schonen, kamm er ~~mir~~ fast meiner jezigen natürlichen Disposizion entgegen, obschon, Vom Triebe zur Gesellschaft manchmal hingerissen, ich mich dazu verleiten ließ, aber welche Demüthigung wenn jemand neben mir stund und von weitem eine Flöte hörte und **ich nichts** hörte, oder jemand den **Hirten Singen** hörte, und ich auch nichts hörte,

[Second page of the autograph] solche Ereignisse brachten mich nahe an Verzweiflung, es fehlte wenig, und ich endigte selbst mein Leben – nur sie die **Kunst**, sie hielt mich zurück, ach es dünkte mir unmöglich, die Welt eher zu verlassen, bis ich das alles hervorgebracht, wozu ich mich aufgelegt fühlte, und so fristete ich dieses elende Leben – wahrhaft elend, einen so reizbaren Körper, daß eine etwas schnelle Verändrung mich aus dem Besten Zustande in den schlechtesten versezen kann – **Geduld** – so heist es, Sie muß ich nun zur führerin wählen, ich habe es – daurend hoffe ich, soll mein Entschluß seyn, auszuharren, bis es den unerbittlichen Parzen gefällt, den Faden zu brechen, vieleicht geht's besser, vieleicht nicht, ich bin gefaßt – schon in meinem 28 Jahre gezwungen Philosoph zu werden, es ist nicht leicht, für den Künstler schwere[r] als für irgend jemand – Gottheit du siehst herab auf mein inneres, du kennst es, du weist, daß menschenliebe und neigung zum Wohlthun drin Hausen, o Menschen, wenn ihr einst dieses leset, so denkt, daß ihr mir unrecht gethan, und der unglückliche, er tröste sich, einen seines gleichen zu finden, der troz allen Hindernissen der Natur, doch noch alles gethan, was in seinem Vermögen stand, um in die Reihe würdiger Künstler und Menschen aufgenommen zu werden – ihr meine Brüder *Carl* und {Leerraum}, sobald ich Tod bin und Professor schmid lebt noch, so bittet ihn in meinem Namen, daß er meine Krankheit beschreibe, und dieses hier geschriebene Blatt füget ihr dieser meiner Krankengeschichte bey, ~~zu~~ damit wenigstens so viel als möglich die Welt nach meinem Tode mit mir versöhnt werde – zugleich erkläre ich euch beyde hier für ~~meine~~ die Erben

134

des kleinen Vermögens, (wenn man es so nennen kann) von mir, theilt es redlich, und vertragt und helft euch einander, was ihr mir zuwider gethan, das wist ihr, war euch schon längst verziehen, dir Bruder *Carl* danke ich noch in's besondre für deine in dieser leztern spätern Zeit mir bewiesene Anhänglichkeit, Mein Wunsch ist, daß ~~ich~~ euch ein bessers sorgen~~volleres~~loseres Leben, als mir, werde, emphelt euren ~~nach~~ Kindern **Tugend**, sie nur allein kann glücklich machen, nicht Geld, ich spreche aus Erfahrung, sie war es, die mich selbst im Elende gehoben, ihr Danke

[Third page of the autograph] ich nebst meiner Kunst, daß ich durch keinen selbstmord mein Leben endigte – lebt wohl und liebt euch; – allen Freunden danke ich, besonders **fürst *Lichnovski*** und **P[r]ofessor schmidt** – die Instrumente von fürst L.[ichnowsky] wünsche ich, daß sie doch mögen aufbewahrt werden bey einem von euch, doch entstehe deswegen kein Streit unter euch, sobald sie euch aber zu was nüzlicherm dienen können, so verkauft sie nur, wie froh bin ich, wenn ich auch noch unter meinem Grabe euch nüzen kann – so wär's geschehen - mit freuden eil ich dem Tode entgegen – kömmt er früher als ich Gelegenheit gehabt habe, noch alle meine Kunst-Fähigkeiten zu entfalten, so wird er mir troz meinem Harten Schicksaal doch noch zu frühe kommen, und ich würde ihn wohl später wünschen – doch auch dann bin ich zufrieden, befreyt er mich nicht von einem endlosen Leidenden Zustande? – Komm, wann du willst, ich gehe dir muthig entgegen – lebt wohl und Vergeßt mich nicht ganz im Tode, ich habe es um euch verdient, indem ich in meinem Leben oft an euch gedacht, euch glücklich zu machen, seyd es –

Ludwig van Beethowen

Heiglnstadt am 6ten *october* 1802

[Fourth page of the autograph – on the right edge, rotated by 90°]

für meine Brüder *Carl* und   nach meinem Tode zu lesen und zu vollziehen –

[Upside-down text]

Heiglnstadt am 10ten *oktober* 1802 – so nehme ich den Abschied von dir – und zwar traurig – ja dir geliebte Hofnung – die ich mit hieher nahm, wenigstens bis zu einem gewissen Punkte geheilet zu seyn – sie muß mich nun gänzlich verlassen, wie die blätter des Herbstes herabfallen, gewelkt sind, so ist – auch sie für mich dürr geworden, fast wie ich hieher kamm – gehe ich fort – selbst der Hohe Muth – der mich oft in den Schönen

Sommertägen beseelte – er ist verschwunden – o Vorsehung – laß einmal einen reinen Tag **der Freude** mir erscheinen – so lange schon ist der wahren Freude inniger widerhall mir fremd – o wann – o Wann o Gottheit – kann ich im Tempel der Natur und der Menschen ihn wider fühlen – Nie? – nein – o es wäre zu hart

[Translation, rather free in light of the run-on sentences of the German original, by A. S. Haley]

Oh, you people who consider or declare me to be bad-tempered, or peevish, or misanthropic, how unjust you are to me! You do not know the hidden cause of what appears thus to you --- from childhood on my heart and soul sought the gentle expression of good will, and I was ever bent toward the accomplishment of even great deeds, but consider that for six years now an incurable condition, made worse by quack doctors, has beset me, betrayed from one year to the next in the hope of getting better, forced at last to the awareness of a chronic malady (whose cure will perhaps take years, or even be impossible). Born with a fiery and lively temperament, receptive for my part to society's distractions, I had to separate myself early and live my life in solitude. When on occasion I wanted to put myself above all of this, ah, how cruelly was I taken aback by the doubly tragic experience of my poor hearing, while not being able to say to people: 'Speak louder, shout, for I am deaf' – how could I admit the frailty of the **one sense** which by rights in me ought to be more perfect than in others, a sense which I once possessed in the highest perfection, a perfection which certainly few of my calling enjoy, or ever have enjoyed: oh, I cannot do it, so forgive me, when you may see me withdraw from your company, even though I should gladly have mixed among you! My misfortune afflicts me twice as hard, in that I am bound to be misunderstood, and that I shall never experience relaxation with my fellow men, or refined conversations, or any mutual exchange of confidences. I dare mingle in society only to the degree that the utmost necessity demands, and must live as one banished. Should company approach me, I am overcome with a feverish anxiety, lest I be placed in danger of letting my condition be noticed. Thus it was also these last six months, which I have spent in the country, at the urging of my sensible doctor to spare my hearing as much as possible, which indeed agreed with my own inclinations, although sometimes, torn by a desire for company, I have let myself be misled – only what a humiliation it was, when someone standing next to me heard a distant flute while **I** heard **nothing**, or when someone heard the **shepherd singing**, but I again heard nothing.

[Page 2] Such incidents have brought me to the brink of despair; a little more and I would have ended my own life – only she, [my] **art**, she held me back, as it struck me as impossible to leave this world before I had brought forth all that I felt was within me. So I endured this wretched existence, truly miserable for so sensitive a person, whom any rather sudden change can transport from the best mood to the worst --- **Patience** --- they say, is the one whom I must now appoint my guide, I have done so; I hope that my resolve to endure shall be lasting, until it shall please the implacable Fates to break my

thread; perhaps it will get better, perhaps not, I am ready. To be forced already, in my 28th year, to become a philosopher is not easy, and for the artist it is more difficult than for anyone else. Oh God, you look down upon my innermost being, you understand it, you know that love of mankind and an inclination to do good dwell therein. Oh mankind, should you one day read this, so reflect that you have done me wrong, and let him who is unfortunate comfort himself to have found his like, who despite all the handicaps of his nature yet did everything in his ability to be accepted into the ranks of worthy artists and men. Oh Carl my brother, and   , so soon as I am dead, if Professor Schmidt is still alive, please ask him in my name to write up a description of my infirmity, and add to his history what I have written here, so that, at the very least, the world may, as much as possible, be reconciled to me after my death. At the same time, I declare you both hereby the heirs of my small estate (if one may so call it): share it honestly, bear with and help each other. Whatever injury you have done me you know has long since been forgiven; you, brother Carl, I thank especially for the devotion you have shown me of late. It is my wish that yours will be a better and more carefree life than mine, that you recommend **Virtue** to your children – that alone, not money, can make them happy—I speak from experience: it was virtue who sustained me in my misery; to her I give thanks,
[Page 3] next to my Art, that I did not end my life by my own hand – farewell and love one another; ---I thank all friends, especially **Prince Lichnowsky** and **Professor Schmidt**. I wish that one of you take care of the instruments from Prince L., but let no argument on their account come between you, and as soon as they might help you obtain something more useful, by all means sell them – how happy shall I be, if even though in my Grave I may still be able to help you both! So be it – I hasten toward my death with glad heart: should it come before I have the opportunity to unfold all of my artistic capabilities, then it will come too early, despite my harsh fate; and even though I might well wish it later, shouldn't I be content if it frees me from a state of endless suffering? Come when you will, [death,] I shall meet you resolutely. Farewell, and do not forget me entirely when I am dead; I deserve that from you, since while alive I thought often of you, and of ways to make you happy – be ye so.

                                                      Ludwig van Beethoven

Heiligenstadt, the 6th October 1802

[Page 4] [On the right edge; text rotated by 90°]

For my brothers Carl and   , to read and carry out after my death –

138

[Upside-down text]

Heiligenstadt, the 10th October 1802 – so I take my leave of you, sad, to be sure – yes you, cherished hope, which I brought here with me, of being healed at least to a certain degree, you also must leave me entirely. As the leaves of autumn fall and wither, so too is my hope blighted. Almost as I came here, so I depart – even that noble courage, that oft in the beautiful days of summer inspired me, has vanished. Oh Providence, let just once a **day of pure joy** appear for me – it is so long now that the inner resonance of true joy has grown foreign to me. Oh, when, when, o God, will I be able to feel that again, in the temple of nature and of mankind – never? No – it would be too hard.

REFERENCES

Abbreviations of Standard Works

BGA   Brandenburg, Sieghard, ed. 1996—. *Ludwig van Beethoven. Briefwechsel: Gesamtausgabe.* Beethovenhaus Bonn (München: G. Henle Verlag). Citations are to the number of each letter (*e.g.*, "BGA No. 140").

BJB   Beethoven-Jahrbuch. 1954-1983, vols. 1-10. Bonn: Beethovenhaus.

Eroica (sketchbook) *See* N 1880; Lockwood & Gosman (ed.) 2013.

Kessler (sketchbook)   *See* N 1865; Brandenburg (ed.) 1978.

JTW   Johnson, Douglas, Alan Tyson and Robert Winter. 1970. *The Beethoven sketchbooks: History, reconstruction, inventory.* Berkeley and Los Angeles: University of California Press.

KBK   Klein, Hans-Günter, ed. 1975. *Ludwig van Beethoven: Autographe und Abschriften.* In: Rudolph Elvers, ed. Staatsbibliotek der Preussischer Kulturbesitz, *Kataloge der Musikabteilung, Erste Reihe: Handschriften, Band 2.* Berlin: Merseburger.

KH   Kinsky, Georg. 1955. *Das Werk Beethovens: Thematisch-bibliograph-isches Verzeichnis sämtlichen vollendeten Kompositionen,* completed and ed. Hans Halm. Munich and Duisberg: G. Henle Verlag.

Landsberg (No.) 6 (sketchbook)   *See* N 1880; Lockwood & Gosman (ed.) 2013.

Landsberg (No.) 7 (sketchbook)   *See* Mikulicz 1927.

NBJ   Neues Beethoven-Jahrbuch. 1924-1939, vols. 1-9. Augsburg: Benno Filser (1924-30, vols. 1-4); Braunschweig: Henry Litolff (1933-39, vols. 5-9).

N 1865   Gustav Nottebohm, ed. 1865. *Ein Skizzenbuch von Beethoven.* Leipzig: Breitkopf & Härtel. Repr. Mies (ed.) 1924; repr. Sändig, Wiesbaden 1970; Eng. transl. Katz 1979.

N 1880   Gustav Nottebohm, ed. 1880. *Ein Skizzenbuch von Beethoven aus dem Jahre 1803.* Leipzig: Breitkopf & Härtel. Repr. Mies (ed.) 1924; repr. Sändig, Wiesbaden 1970; Eng. transl. Katz 1979.

TDR   Thayer, Alexander Wheelock. *Ludwig van Beethovens Leben.* Vol. I (rev.) continued by Hermann Deiters (Berlin: Breitkopf & Härtel, 1901); vols. IV-V completed by Hugo Riemann (Leipzig: Breitkopf & Härtel, 1907, 1908);   vols. II-III rev. Riemann (Leipzig, 1910, 1911); vol. I (ed. Deiters 1901) rev. Riemann (Leipzig, 1917); vols. II-V reissued (Leipzig, 1923).

Thayer   Thayer, Alexander Wheelock. *Ludwig van Beethovens Leben.* Berlin: Ferdinand Schneider (vol. I, 1866); W. Weber (vols. II-III, 1872, 1879).

Thayer-Forbes   Elliot Forbes, ed. 1967. *Thayer's life of Beethoven.* 2 vols., Princeton: Princeton University Press.

Wegeler/Ries   Wegeler, Franz Gerhard and Ferdinand Ries. 1838. *Biographische Notizen über Ludwig van Beethoven.* Suppl. (*Nachtrag*) Wegeler, 1845. Coblenz: K. Badeker. Eng. transl. Noonan 1988.

Wielhorsky (sketchbook)   *See* Fishman, vols. 1 (facsimile) and 2 (transcription).

Books and Articles

Abraham, Gerald. 1975. Musicology's Language Curtain. *Musical Times* 116 (no. 1591, Sept.), 788-89.

Albrecht, Theodore. 1999. Thayer contra Marx: a warning from 1860. *Beethoven Journal* 14/1 (Summer) 2-8 (Pt. I); 14/2 (Winter), 56-64 (Pt. II).

————, ed. 1996. *Letters to Beethoven and other correspondence.* 3 vols., Lincoln and London: University of Nebraska Press.

Aldrich, Elizabeth. 1997. Social Dancing in Schubert's World. In: Raymond Erickson, ed. *Schubert's Vienna*, 119-40. New Haven and London: Yale University Press.

Applebaum, Stanley. 2002. Introduction to Ludwig van Beethoven, *The creatures of Prometheus, Op. 43, the complete ballet music in full score*. Mineola, NY: Dover Publications, Inc.

Bekker, Paul. 1912. *Beethoven*. 2d. ed., Berlin: Deutsche Verlags-Anstalt.

Bertagnolli, Paul. 2007. *Prometheus in music: representations of the myth in the romantic era*. Aldershot: Ashgate.

Beyle, Marie-Henri [Stendhal]. 1822. *De l'amour*. 2 vols., Paris: P. Mongie l'ainé. 1888. German transl. by Arthur Schurig: *Die Physiologie der Liebe*. Berlin: Fried.

Brandenburg, Sieghard. 1977. Über die Bedeutung der Skizzen Beethovens. In Goldschmidt, Köhler and Niemann (eds.) 1978, 37-63.

———, ed. 1978. *Ludwig van Beethoven: Keßlersches Skizzenbuch*. 2 vols., Bonn: Beethovenhaus.

Brockhaus, Alfred and Konrad Niemann, eds. 1971. *Bericht über den internationalen Beethoven-Kongreß 1970*. Berlin: Verlag Neue Musik.

Brown, Malcolm. 1963. Book review [of Fishman]. *Notes* (Series 2) vol. 20, no. 3 (Summer), 460-63.

Burnham, Scott. 1995. *Beethoven hero*. Princeton: Princeton University Press.

Burnham, Scott and Michael Steinberg, eds. 2000. *Beethoven and his world*. Princeton and Oxford: Princeton University Press.

Carner, Mosco. 1970. Beethoven's deafness and the heroic element in his music. In: Carl Dahlhaus *et al.* (eds.) 1971, 360-61.

Cooper, Barry. 1990. *Beethoven and the creative process*. New York: Oxford University Press.

———. 1995. Beethoven's Oratorio and the Heiligenstadt Testament. *Beethoven Journal* 10/1, 19-24.

————. 1999. Introduction to Urtext Study edition of: Beethoven, L. van. *Symphony no. 3, op. 55 ("Eroica")*. Kassel: Bärenreiter Verlag.

————. 2000a. *Beethoven*. Oxford: Oxford University Press.

————. 2000b. The compositional act: sketches and autographs. In Glenn Stanley, ed. *The Cambridge companion to Beethoven*, 32-42. Cambridge: Cambridge University Press.

Dahlhaus, Carl. 1987. *Ludwig van Beethoven und seine Zeit*. Laaber: Laaber-Verlag. 1991. Eng. transl. by Mary Whittall: *Ludwig van Beethoven – Approaches to his music*. Oxford: Clarendon Press.

————, *et al.*, eds. 1971. *Bericht über den Internationalen Musikwissenschaftlichen Kongress Bonn 1970*. Kassel: Bärenreiter-Verlag.

Dean, Winton. 1969. *Handel and the opera seria*. Berkeley and Los Angeles: University of California Press.

Derr, Ellwood. 1984. Beethoven's long-term memory of C.P.E. Bach's Rondo in E-Flat, W. 61/1 (1787), manifest in the Variations in E-Flat for Piano, Opus 35 (1802). *Musical Quarterly* 70, 45-76.

Dorfmüller, Kurt, ed. 1978. *Beiträge zur Beethoven-Bibliographie: Studien und Materialen zum Werkverzeichnis von Kinsky-Halm*. Munich: G. Henle Verlag.

Fischer, K. von. 1949. Eroica-Variationen Op. 35 und Eroica-Finale. *Schweizerische Musikzeitung* 89, 282-86.

Fischman [German transliteration of "Fishman"], Nathan. 1970. Das Skizzenbuch Beethovens aus den Jahren 1802-1803 aus dem Familienarchiv Wielhorski und die ersten Skizzen zur 'Eroica'. In Dahlhaus *et al.* (eds.) 1971, 104-07.

————. 1978. Das Moskauer Skizzenbuch Beethovens aus dem Archiv von M. J. Wielhorsky. In Dorfmüller (ed.) 1978, 61-67.

Fishman, Nathan L., ed. 1962 (cited as "Fishman"). *Kniga èskizov Betxovena za 1802-1803 gody*, 3 vols. (facsimile, transcription and commentary). Moscow: Gosudarstvennoj

Muzykal'noj Izdatel'stvo (State Musical Press).

Fleischhauer, Günter. 1970. Beethoven und die Antike. In: Brockhaus and Niemann (eds.) 1971, 465-482.

Floros, Constantin. 1978. *Beethovens Eroica und Prometheus-Musik.* Wilhelmshaven: Heinrichshofens Verlag.

————. 2008. *Beethovens Eroica und Prometheus-Musik. Sujet-Studien.* Wilhelmshaven: Florian Noetzel Verlag, Heinrichshofen Books. Eng. tr. by Ernest Bernhardt-Kabisch, 2013. *Beethoven's Eroica. Thematic Studies.* Frankfurt: Peter Lang GmbH.

Gleich, Clemens-Christoph von. 1996. *Beethovens Prometheus-Variationen in Neuer Sicht.* Munich-Salzburg: Musikverlag Emil Katzbichler.

Goldschmidt, Harry. 1975. *Beethoven – Werkeinführungen.* Leipzig: Verlag P. Reclam jun.

Goldschmidt, Harry, Karl-Heinz Köhler and Konrad Niemann, eds. 1978. *Bericht über den Internationalen Beethoven-Kongreß Berlin 1977.* Leipzig: VEB Deutscher Verlag für Musik.

Grout, Donald Jay. 1965. *A short history of opera.* 2d ed. New York and London: Columbia University Press.

Grove, George. 1898. *Beethoven and his nine symphonies.* 3d. ed. London: Novello, Ewer and Co. 1962. Repr. New York: Dover Publications, Inc.

Haag, John J. 1990. Beethoven, the revolution in music, and the French revolution: music and politics in Austria, 1790-1815, in: Brauer, Kinley and William E. Wright, eds. *Austria in the age of the French revolution 1790-1815.* Minneapolis: Center for Austrian Studies (University of Minnesota), 107-123.

Haas, Robert. 1925. Zur Wiener Ballettpantomime um den Prometheus. *Neues Beethoven-Jahrbuch* 2, 84-103.

Haas, Robert. 1927. Beethoven und das Wiener Ballett. *Velhagen & Klasings Monatshefte* 41/7 (March), 41-48.

Haley, Allan S. 1966. *Beethoven: the Sketchbook for 1802-1803*. Unpublished honors thesis (2 vols.) in the Eda Kuhn Loeb Music Library of Harvard University.

Hamilton-Paterson, James. 2017. *Beethoven's Eroica – the First Great Romantic Symphony*. New York: Basic Books.

Heineman, Michael. 1992. "Altes" und "Neues" in Beethovens "Eroica"-Variationen op. 35. *Archiv für Musikwissenschaft* 49/1, 38-45.

Hess, Willy. 1962. *Beethovens Bühnenwerke*. Göttingen: Vandenhoeck & Ruprecht.

Hess, Willy, ed. 1939. Introduction to: *Nei giorni tuoi felici aus "Olimpiade" Akt I, Szene 10 von Pietro Metastasio: Duett für Sopran und Tenor mit Orchester / von Ludwig van Beethoven; nach dem in der Preussichen Staatsbibliothek befindlichen Autograph zum ersten Male hrsg. und zum Vortrag eingerichtet* (WoO 93; in miniature score). Leipzig: E. Eulenberg.

Johnson, Douglas. 1978. Beethoven scholars and Beethoven's sketches. *19th Century Music* 2, no. 1 (July), 3-17.

Katz, Jonathan, trans. 1979. *Two Beethoven sketchbooks: A description with musical extracts, by Gustav Nottebohm*. London: Gollancz.

Kerényi, Carl. 1959. *Prometheus: Die menschliche Existenz in griechischer Deutung*. Hamburg: Rowohlt Verlag. 1963. Eng. trans. *Prometheus – Archetypal image of human existence*. Princeton: Princeton University Press.

Kerman, Joseph, ed. 1970. *Ludwig van Beethoven: Autograph miscellany from circa 1786 to 1799*. 2 vols., London: Oxford University Press for the Trustees of the British Museum.

Kinderman, William. 1995. *Beethoven*. Oxford: Oxford University Press.

———, 2009 (2d ed.). *Beethoven*. Oxford: Oxford University Press.

———, ed. 1991. *Beethoven's compositional process*. North American Beethoven Studies, vol.

I. Lincoln & London: University of Nebraska Press.

Kinsky, Georg. 1935. Zur Versteigerung von Beethovens musikalischem Nachlaß. *NBJ* 6, 66-86.

Kloiber, Rudolph. 1973. *Handbuch der Oper I.* 8th ed., Munich: Deutsche Taschenbuch Verlag.

Kojima, Shin August. 1977. Zweifelhafte Authentizität einiger Beethoven zugeschriebene Orchestertänze. In: Goldschmidt, Köhler and Niemann (eds.) 1978, 307-22.

Kojima, Shin August, ed. 1980. Kritischer Bericht for BWG Abt. II, Bd. 3: *Gratulationsmenuett und Tänze für Orchester.* Beethovenhaus Bonn (Munich: G. Henle Verlag).

Knight, Frida. 1973. *Beethoven and the age of revolution.* London: Lawrence & Wishart.

Kunze, Stefan. 1972. Die "wirklich gantz neue Manier" in Beethovens Eroica-Variationen op. 35. *Archiv für Musikwissenchaft* 29/2, 124-49.

Lang, Paul, ed. 1971. *The creative world of Beethoven.* New York: W.W. Norton & Co.

Lenz, Wilhelm von. 1852. *Beethoven et ses trois stiles.* St. Petersburg: Bernard.

Lenz, Wilhelm von. 1855/60. *Beethoven: Eine Kunststudie.* Kassel: Ernst Balde, 1855 (vols. I & II); Hamburg: Hoffman & Campe, 1860 (vol. III).

Lenz, Wilhelm von. 1856. Graf Mikhail Jur'evich Wielhorsky. In German; trans. into Russian by A.N. Serov, in *Muzykal'nyj i teatral'nyj vestnik*, No. 49, p. 882.

Levinson, A. 1927. Le Ballet de Promethée, Beethoven et Vigano. *Revue de Musique* 8, 87-97.

Linton, Patricia. 2004. Ballet's Beginnings. *Dancing Times* (January), 94-95.

Lockwood, Lewis. 1970. On Beethoven's sketches and autographs: Some problems of definition and interpretation. *Acta Musicologica* XLII: 32-47. Reprinted in Lockwood 1992, 4-16.

————. 1981. The earliest sketches for the Eroica symphony. *Musical Quarterly* 67, 457-78. Reprinted in Lockwood 1992, 134-50.

————. 1991. The compositional genesis of the *Eroica* finale. In: Kinderman (ed.) 1991, 82-101. Repr. in Lockwood 1992, at 151-166.

————. 1992. *Beethoven – Studies in the creative process.* Cambridge, Massachusetts and London, England: Harvard University Press.

————. 2000. Beethoven, Florestan and the varieties of heroism. In: Burnham and Steinberg (eds.) 2000, 27-47.

————. 2003. *Beethoven – The music and the life.* New York and London: W.W. Norton & Co.

Lockwood, Lewis and Alan Gosman, eds. 2013. *Beethoven's "Eroica" sketchbook: a critical edition.* Vol. 1 (commentary/transcription); Vol.2 (facsimile). Urbana, Chicago and Springfield: University of Illinois Press.

MacArdle, Donald W., ed. 1996. *Beethoven as I knew him* [Transl of Schindler 1860]. Mincola, NY: Dover Publications.

Maruyama, Keisuke. 1987. Die Sinfonie des Prometheus. *Beethoven / Analecta Varia* 56 (July), 46-82. Munich: Johannesdruck Hans Pribil KG.

Marx, Adolph Bernhard. 1859. *Ludwig van Beethoven: Leben und Schaffen.* 2 vols., Berlin: Verlag Otto Janke. 1863. 2d. ed., 2 vols.

Massin, Jean and Brigitte. 1970. Beethoven et la Révolution Française, in: *Beethoven.* Aix-en-Provence: L'Arc, No. 1375, 1er trimestre, 3-14.

Mathew, Nicholas and Benjamin Walton, eds. 2013. *The Invention of Beethoven and Rossini: Historiography, Analysis, Criticism.* Cambridge: Cambridge University Press.

Mathews, Denis. 1985. *Beethoven.* Oxford: Oxford University Press.

Mies, Paul. 1925. *Die Bedeutung der Skizzen Beethovens zur Erkenntnis seines Stiles.* Leipzig:

Breitkopf & Härtel. 1929. Eng. transl. by Doris Mackinnon: *Beethoven's sketches – An analysis of his style based on a study of his sketch-books*. Oxford: Oxford University Press. Repr. 1974. New York: Dover Publications.

————. 1953-54. Ludwig van Beethovens Werke über seinen Kontretanz in Es-Dur. BJB 1, 80-102. Bonn: Beethovenhaus.

————, ed. 1924. *Zwei Skizzenbücher von Beethoven aus den Jahren 1801 bis 1803. Beschrieben und in Auszügen dargestellt von Gustav Nottebohm*. Leipzig: Breitkopf & Härtel. Repr. Sändig 1970.

Mikulicz, Karl, ed. 1927. *Ein Notierungsbuch von Beethoven*. Leipzig: Breitkopf & Härtel.

Morris, Edmund. 2005. *Beethoven the universal composer*. New York: Harper Collins.

Müller, Erich Hermann. 1929. Beethoven und Simrock. *Simrock-Jahrbuch* 2, 27ff.

Nohl, Ludwig. 1874. *Beethoven, Liszt, Wagner*. Vienna: Wilhelm Braumüller.

Noli, Fan S. (Bishop). 1947. *Beethoven and the French revolution*. New York: International Universities Press.

Noonan, Frederick, trans. 1987. *Remembering Beethoven: the biographical notes of Franz Wegeler and Ferdinand Ries / foreword by Christopher Hogwood, introduction by Eva Badura-Skoda*. London: Andre Deutsch. (US ed. publ. 1988 as *Beethoven remembered*, Arlington, VA: Great Ocean Publishers.) Trans. of 1906 Berlin ed. of Wegeler/Ries with notes by Alfred Kalischer.

Nottebohm, Gustav. 1868. *Thematisches Verzeichniss der im Druck erschienenen Werke von Ludwig van Beethoven*. 2d. ed., Leipzig: Breitkopf & Härtel.

Paunel, Eugen von and Gustav Gugitz, ed. 1917-18. *Die Eipeldauer Briefe 1799-1813 in Auswahl herausgegeben*. 2 vols., Munich: Georg Müller. Selections from Richter 1785-1813.

Pichler, Caroline. 1844. *Denkwürdigkeiten aus meinem Leben*. 4 vols. (in 2), Vienna: Verlag von A. Pichlers sel. Witwe.

Pichler, Ernst. 1994. *Beethoven – Mythos und Wirklichkeit.* Vienna and Munich: Amalthea Verlag.

Reichart, Sarah Bennett. 1984. *The influence of eighteenth-century social dance on Viennese classical style.* Ph.D. diss., City University of New York.

Reizler, Walter. 1990. *Beethoven.* 13th ed., Zürich: Atlantis Musikbuch Verlag.

Reynolds, Christopher. 1982. Beethoven's sketches for the Variations in E-Flat Op. 35. In: Alan Tyson, ed. *Beethoven Studies 3*, 47-74. Cambridge: Cambridge University Press.

Rice, John A. 2003. *Empress Marie Therese and music at the Viennese court 1792-1807.* Cambridge: Cambridge University Press.

Richter, Joseph. 1785-1813. *Eipeldauer-Briefe (Briefe eines Eipeldauers an seinen Herrn Vetter in Kakran über d' Wienstadt).* Vienna: J. Richter. Selections reprinted in Paunel and Gugitz, ed. 1917-18.

Riemann, Hugo. 1909-10. Beethovens Prometheus-Musik. Ein Variationenwerk. *Die Musik 8*, 19-34, 107-125.

Ringer, Alexander. 1961. Clementi and the *Eroica. Musical Quarterly* 47, 454-68.

Ritorni, Carlo. 1838. *Commentaria della vita e delle opere corredrammatiche di Salvatore di Viganò e della corregrafia e de' corporei scritti.* Milan: Reggiano.

Rolland, Romain. 1928. *Beethoven - les grandes époques créatrices: De l'Héroique à l'Appassionata.* Paris: Editions du Sablier. 1929. Eng. tr. by Ernest Newman: *Beethoven the creator.* London: Victor Gollanz. Repr. 1964. New York: Dover Publications.

Rumph, Stephen. 2004. *Beethoven after Napoleon.* Berkeley and Los Angeles: University of California Press.

Sändig, Martin. 1970. Reprint of Mies (ed.) 1924. Wiesbaden: Dr. Martin Sändig oHG.

Schenker, Heinrich. 1930. *Das Meisterwerk in der Musik*. Vol. 3, Munich: Drei Masken Verlag.

Schindler, Anton. 1840. *Biographie von Ludwig van Beethoven*. Münster: Aschendorff'schen Buchhandlung. 1845. 2nd ed., 2 vols. 1860. 3d ed. (*Dritte, neu bearbeitete und vermehrte Auflage*), 2 vols. English tr. of 3d ed.: MacArdle (ed.) 1996.

Schleuning, Peter. 1987. Beethoven in alter Deutung: Der 'neue Weg' mit der Sinfonia Eroica. *Archiv für Musikwissenschaft* 44, 165-94.

————. 1996. 3. Symphonie Es-Dur. In: Albrecht Riethmüller, Carl Dahlhaus and Alexander Ringer, eds. *Beethoven – Interpretationen seiner Werke*. 2d ed., Laaber: Laaber-Verlag, vol. I, 386-400.

———— and Martin Geck. 1989. *"Geschrieben auf Bonaparte."* Reinbek bei Hamburg: Rowohlt Taschenbuch Verlag.

Schmitz, Arnold. 1927. *Beethoven*. Bonn: Verlag der Buchgemeinde.

Schneider, Frank. 1988. *Welt, was frag ich nach dir?* Leipzig: Verlag Philipp Reclam jun.

Schüller, Gunhild, and Thomas Steiert. 1997. Salvatore Viganò--Raul, Herr von Krecki. *Pipers Enzyklopedie des Musiktheaters.* Munich: Piper Verlag, vol. VI, pp. 497-500.

Schwarz, Boris. 1961. Beethoveniana in Soviet Russia. 47 *Musical Quarterly* 4-21.

Senner, Wayne M., Robin Wallace and William Meredith, eds. 1999 (vol. 1) and 2001 (vol. 2). *The critical reception of Beethoven's compositions by his German contemporaries.* 2 vols., Lincoln and London: University of Nebraska Press.

Sipe, Thomas. 1998. *Beethoven:* Eroica *Symphony*. Cambridge: Cambridge University Press.

Smart, Mary Ann. 2013. Beethoven dances: Prometheus and his creatures in Vienna and Milan. In: Mathew and Walton (eds.) 2013, 210-35.

Smolle, Kurt. 1970. *Wohnstätten Ludwig van Beethovens von 1792 bis zu seinem Tod.*

Beethovenhaus Bonn (München-Duisberg: G. Henle Verlag).

Solomon, Maynard. 1977. Beethoven – Class position and outlook. In: Goldschmidt, Köhler and Niemann (eds.) 1978, 67-79.fere

————. 1998. *Beethoven.* 2d ed., New York: Schirmer Books.

Sonnleithner, L. 1861. Beethoven's Musik zu dem Prometheus-Ballett. *Niederrheinischer Musikzeitung für Kunstfreunde und Künstler* 79, 85-87, 94-95.

Stendhal. *See* Beyle, Marie-Henri.

Sullivan, J.W.N. 1927. *Beethoven – His spiritual development.* New York: New American Library. Repr. 1960. New York: Vintage Books.

Swafford, Jan. 2014. *Beethoven – Anguish and Triumph.* New York: Houghton Mifflin Harcourt.

Syer, Katherine. 2006. A peculiar hybrid: The structure and chronology of the "Eroica" sketchbook. *Bonner Beethoven-Studien* 5, 159-81. Bonn: Beethovenhaus.

Thürheim, Lulu (Gräfin). 1788-1852. *Ma vie.* René van Rhyn, trans. and ed. 1913-14. *Mein Leben. Erinnerungen aus Österreichs grosser Welt 1788-1819 /1819-1852.* 4 vols., Munich: Georg Müller.

Trousson, Raymond. 2001. *La thème de Promethée dans la littérature européenne.* 3d ed. Geneva: Librairie Droz.

Tusa, Michael. 1985. Die authentischen Quellen der "Eroica". *Archiv für Musikwissenschaft* 42/2, 121-150.

Tyson, Alan. 1969. Beethoven's Heroic Phase. *Musical Times* CX, 139-141.

Tyson, Alan. 1970. The 1803 version of Beethoven's *Christus am Oelberge.* 56 *Musical Quarterly* 551-84. Reprinted in Lang (ed.) 1971, 49-82.

Volek, Tomislav and Jaroslav Macek. 1986. Beethoven's rehearsals at the Lobkowitz's,

Musical Times 127, no. 1716 (February), 75-80.

Voss, Egon and Gunhild Schüller. 1997. Salvatore Viganò – Die Geschöpfe des Prometheus. *Pipers Enzyklopedie des Musiktheaters.* Munich: Piper Verlag, vol. VI, pp. 500-503.

Wade, Rachel. 1977. Beethoven's *Eroica* sketchbook. *Fontes Artis Musicae* 24, 254-73.

Walzel, Oskar. 1932. *Das Prometheussymbol von Shaftesbury zu Goethe.* 2d ed. Munich: Max Huber Verlag.

Weissensteiner, Friedrich. 2001. *Die österreichischen Kaiserinnen 1804-1918.* Munich: Piper Verlag.

Witte, Reinhard. 2003. Beethoven, Homer und die Antike. *Das Altertum* 48/1, 3-54.

Würz, Anton and Reinhold Schimkat, eds. 1961. *Beethoven in Briefen und Lebens-Dokumenten.* Stuttgart: Philipp Reclam jun.

Zanden, Jos van der. 2005. Ferdinand Ries in Wien – Neue Perspektiven zu den *Notizen. Bonner Beethoven-Studien* 4, 191-212. Bonn: Beethovenhaus.

ENDNOTES

[1] The other is, of course, the Sixth Symphony, which Beethoven christened *"Sinfonia Pastoral"*.

[2] For a survey of the known sketchbooks, *see* JTW, especially 1-43. For a description of how Beethoven used sketchbooks in the compositional process, and their significance for Beethoven studies, *see* Brandenburg 1977 and Cooper 2000b.

[3] *See* the useful discussion of autographs vs. sketches in Lockwood 1970 (repr. Lockwood 1992, pp. 4ff). The autograph scores in the Beethoven collection of the German State Library are described in KBK.

[4] *See* Smolle 1970.

[5] *See* Kinsky 1935; JTW 13-19 (auctioning of the sketchbooks).

[6] Mikhail Jur'evich Wielhorsky [or in stricter transliteration, "Wiel'gorskij"] (1787-1856), who had met Beethoven on a visit to Vienna in 1808 and became a promoter of his works in Russia. *See* Fishman, vol. III, 39-40, where he cites an article (Lenz 1856) that credits Count Wielhorsky with being the first to distinguish the so-called "three styles" of Beethoven.

[7] No general discussions of the sketchbook in English have appeared apart from Schwarz 1961, Brown 1963 and JTW, 130-36; *see also* Abraham 1975, to which this study is in part a response. Sketches which the book contains for individual works have been discussed and analyzed in the articles and books cited below; *see also* the discussions in Tyson 1970; and the pages indexed under "SV 343" in Cooper 1990, 316. Nathan Fishman has also published two brief articles in German summarizing his findings regarding the

sketchbook: Fischman 1970 and Fischman 1978.

[8] It is a mistake to do so, as explained in the text at p. 40, n. 108.

[9] *See* pages 44-45 of the Wielhorsky sketchbook as transcribed by Fishman, reproduced herein as Plates 14 and 15, *and see* the fuller discussion in ch. 6 at 57-64.

[10] *See, e.g.,* Nohl 1874, 98-99; Fishman, Vol. III, 110ff; Lockwood 1981; Cooper 2000a, 129-30. *(inadequate?)*

[11] *See* the discussion at 61-63.

[12] BGA No. 140 (undated), which editor Sieghard Brandenburg believes was written at the end of May or the beginning of June in 1803 (p. 167, n.1). The Italian title was translated first into German as "*Die Menschen des Prometheus*", then—just a week before the ballet's opening—it was changed to "*Die Geschöpfe des Prometheus*" (*see* n. 40). It is from the latter title that the English title most commonly associated with the work is derived: "*The Creatures of Prometheus*", with "creatures of P." understood in the sense of "humans created by P." The Italian "*uomini*" means "men"; "humans" would be "*umani*". In German, however, "*Menschen*" has both meanings, while "*Geschöpfe*" has the broader connotation of "creatures", or "things created". Since Prometheus created one human of each gender, a literal translation of the Italian has never seemed appropriate for the work.

[13] *See* chapter 4, at 31ff.

[14] *Zwölf Contretänze für Orchester* (WoO 14), first published in 1802 (KH 449-51).

[15] *E.g.,* Grove (repr.) 1962, 58-60, 93; Bekker 1912, 216. Mozart was twelve when he wrote *Bastien et Bastienne* in 1768 for the renowned Viennese hypnotist, Dr. Franz Anton Mesmer. The work, which is only 35 minutes or so in duration, appears to have been given a single performance in the garden Marionettentheater (puppet theater) at Dr. Mesmer's home. It is not known to have been performed elsewhere, or to have been published, until after its rediscovery in connection with the Mozart Zentenarfeier in Vienna in 1891. (*See* Kloiber 1973, at 315.) The contrast between the formal manner in which the twelve-year-old Mozart uses the theme in the opera's short *intrada* and the organic way in which Beethoven uses it to engender a complete symphonic movement

(which lasts almost as long as Mozart's entire opera!) could not be more striking. As will be shown by the evidence to be reviewed in this book, Beethoven evolved the theme linearly, out of his work on the piano variations op. 35, and thus, apart from the difficulty in envisioning how Beethoven could even have been aware of Mozart's once-performed *Singspiel*, it can be concluded only that the similarity between the two works is sheer coincidence. As Lewis Lockwood stated after examining the Beethoven's early sketches for the Symphony, ". . . even now this myth [of Beethoven borrowing from Mozart] dies hard in some quarters, but it surely can be laid to rest for good." Lockwood 1981, at 469, repr. Lockwood 1992, at 144.

[16] *See* Ringer 1961, esp. 457-58. Needless to say, just as in the case of Mozart, the same considerations furnished by the sketches negate any conscious borrowing from Clementi. Subconsciously, the case fares no better, since the character of the theme in Clementi's hands is so very different: it is in G minor, not E-Flat Major (although the passage quoted in Fig. 2 is over an E-flat pedal-point); melodically it is not the same, and the feature that most links Beethoven's theme with its bass—the ascent to the fifth, as its climax—is wholly missing in Clementi, whose theme descends throughout. (*Compare* Fig. 2 *with* Fig. 16 below.) Similarly, the hypothesis of Derr (1984) (stated by his article's title) relates chiefly to keyboard similarities between the two works mentioned. It does not take into account the genesis of the ballet or the contredanse; the similarities that Derr points out could well have arisen while Beethoven was composing variations for the piano, without saying anything about how the theme evolved out of his work on the ballet.

[17] The last pages in the Wielhorsky sketchbook contain sketches for the first two movements of the "Kreutzer" violin sonata, op. 47, which Beethoven first performed with the British violinist George Bridgetower on May 24, 1803. *See* the discussion of the determination of the sequence Kessler-Wielhorsky-*Eroica* in the text at nn. 128-34 (pp. 49-51); *see also* JTW, 125-28 (Kessler), 133-34 (Wielhorsky), and 139-43 ("*Eroica*" [Landsberg 6]); *but see* n. 155, and Syer 2006.

[18] Letter from Ferdinand Ries to Nikolaus Simrock (first published in Müller 1929, 27f), BGA No. 165. Müller gives the date of the letter as October 22, 1803, but the location of the original is now (after World War II) unknown.

[19] *See* Wegeler/Ries, 77-79; Eng. Tr., pp. 68-69.

[20] Haley 1966. This book reproduces (and updates) most of what that thesis had to say about the genesis of the *Eroica* Symphony.

[21] I have tried to credit each individual contribution of which I am aware in this book, and have cited the sources as they are relevant on individual points. To anyone whom I happen to have overlooked, my apologies.

[22] In a letter written from Vienna on March 7, 1801, Caspar Josef Eberl, the local representative of the publishers Hoffmeister & Kühnel in Leipzig, reported to his home office: "I spoke with Beethoven on the first of this month, and received in response that since he has obtained work to do at present from her Majesty the Empress, he will not be in a position for the next 14 days to do anything, whether for himself or for anyone else. . .". ("am ersten dies hab ich mit H. *v Beethoven* gesprochen und in antworth erhalten, da er von S.<u>r</u> *Majestät* der Kays.[Kaiserin] *presante* arbeit bekommen, so ist er vor 14 Taagen nicht im Stande weder für sich noch für andere was zu thuen . . .".) BGA No. 57; the letter thus would lead one to believe that the commission came to Beethoven directly from the Empress, as opposed to through the dance director for the Imperial Theater, Salvatore Viganò. Since the latter's duties charged him to perform each year a new work of his own choreography, however (*see* n. 31), and since *Prometheus* was the third in the series of ballets Viganò created in satisfaction of this obligation, it is likely that it was within the scope of his duties to select a composer for each new work as well. Provided the selection was agreeable to the court, presumably a commission would issue under the imperial seal. The letter shows how Beethoven regarded his work as being done for Marie Therese herself, and how he consequently gave it top priority. (*See also* the confirmation of Marie Therese's connection to the ballet by Viganò's biographer Carlo Ritorni [App. C at p. 96, last paragraph].) On the musical influence of Marie Therese at the court of Franz II, *see* Rice 2003.

[23] On Viganò's biography and ballets, *see* Ritorni 1838; TDR II, 216ff.; Applebaum 2002, pp. vi-vii; Schüller and Steiert 1997; Levinson 1927; Haas 1927 (with useful illustrations); Haas 1925.

[24] As pointed out by Applebaum (2002), at ix, n. 3.

[25] Prior to the *ballet d'action,* ballet was a stilted, formal affair, with the dancers attired in masks and bulky costumes that restricted their movement. Modern ballet dress came in

with the *ballet d'action*, which required the dancers to be far more active. *See* the description of the older style by Heinrich Josef von Collin referenced in n. 29.

[26] Josepha Maria Medina was born with the surname Meyerin in Vienna in 1756. Haas 1925, at 97 (note, however, that the editor of Gräfin Lulu Thürheim's diary (Thürheim 1913) gives her name as "Josefa Meyer"). *See* Plates 3-4.

[27] Stendhal (drawing on contemporary descriptions from the *Eipeldauerbriefe* [Richter 1785-1813]), observed: "A Vienne, en 1788, Mme Viganò . . . ("A dancer in Vienna, Madame Viganò, who was at that time very much in fashion, came into different circumstances in the year 1788---no sooner had she done so, than the ladies began to wear waistlines [*kleine Bäuche*, literally "little bellies"] à la Viganò." The passage in the German translation reads: "Eine Tänzerin in Wien, Madame Viganò, die damals sehr in Mode war, kam im Jahre 1788 in andere Umstände, – und alsbald trugen die Damen kleine Bäuche à la Viganò.") (Beyle 1822, Ger. Trans. 1888), ch. 18. Stendhal is of course wrong with his date, since that was the earliest year that Viganò could have *met* his future wife---in Spain. Madame Viganò did not make her first appearance on a Viennese stage until May 13, 1793 (TDR II, 216).

[28] In 1795, Ludwig van Beethoven composed a set of variations on a "Menuett à la Viganò" which had appeared in a ballet by Chechi with music by Mozart's brother-in-law, Jakob Haibel (WoO 68; *see* KH 517-18). It may have been this composition which brought the young composer to Viganò's attention.

[29] *See* TDR II, 217f. for an account of the controversy based on a description by the playwright Heinrich Josef von Collin (author of *Coriolan*).

[30] So suggests Gräfin Lulu Thürheim in her memoirs (Thürheim 1788-1852), vol. I, pp. 126-27. She adds that Marie Therese's response to the affair was not subtle: "Once, as the Emperor showed a decided preference for a dancer, Madam Viganò, the Empress had a statue made of her and erected it in a spot in Laxenburg Park; its costume and figure were true to nature in representing the ballerina, but in place of its head she had them put the skull of a billy goat." ("Als einst eine Tänzerin Frau Viganò vom Kaiser sehr bevorzugt wurde, ließ [die Kaiserin] deren Statue anfertigen und stellte sie auf einen Platz im Laxenburger Park; Kostüm und Gestalt waren in naturgetreuer Darstellung die der Tänzerin, nur an Stelle des Kopfes ließ sie den Schädel eines Ziegenbockes setzen.")

[31] Applebaum 2002, at vii. Perhaps, given Marie Therese's attitude toward Maria Viganò (n. 30), she induced Sgr. Viganò to return to Vienna with the offer of a contract, now that his former wife was no longer a threat to her.

[32] Rice (2003), at 246-48, thinks that Beethoven gave Empress Marie Therese the manuscript of his Septet for her exclusive use for two years, before its publication and official dedication to her. If so, that could provide the motive for commissioning the music for the ballet from him.

[33] Massin 1970; Knight 1973, chs. 1-5; Haag 1990; Noli 1947.

[34] Weissensteiner 2001, 27-30.

[35] Symphony No. 1 in C Major, op. 21; Piano Concerto No. 1 in C Major, op. 15, and No. 2 in B-Flat Major, op. 19; Six String Quartets, op. 18; Septet in E-Flat Major, op. 20. While none of these works had been published as of early 1801, they had all been performed in public, and had been the subject of numerous reviews.

[36] Hess 1962, 11-25.

[37] BGA No. 57, quoted in n. 22.

[38] *See* Plate 6, p. 11. The opening, however, was postponed until March 28, ostensibly due to Beethoven's illness (Voss and Schüller 1997, 501).

[39] Voss and Schüller 1997; *see* text in connection with Fig. 4 at p. 22-24.

[40] The contents of the announcement are reprinted in TDR II, 220 and Plate 6. In another last-minute decision, Viganò changed the name of the work to *Die Geschöpfe des Prometheus,* ostensibly in an attempt to capitalize on the great success of Haydn's oratorio *Die Schöpfung,* selections from which had been regularly performed in Vienna since its premiere in 1798. As noted earlier (n. 12), this change determined how the work would be referred to thereafter in English, despite its title in Italian.

[41] Reprinted in TDR II, 219 and Plate 7.

[42] Ritorni 1838, at 47-50. The relevant pages of this very rare book are reproduced in Plates 8 and 9 (*see* Appendix C, at pp. 93-94). TDR II, 221-22 gives a German translation; both Floros 1978 and Maruyama 1987 give parallel versions in Italian and German. An English translation appears in Sipe 1998 (Appendix, at 117-18); however, it needs correction, and also does not include Ritorni's critical remarks. In Appendix C (pp. 95-96), I give my own translation of the commentary into English.

[43] "Die Geschöpfe des Prometheus", *Zeitung für die elegante Welt I* (April 1801), 485-87 (quoted at pp. 19-20 [German text in App. D, at pp. 97-98]) (English tr.: Senner, Wallace and Meredith [eds.] 1999, at 215-16); *Journal des Luxus und der Moden* 16 (Weimar, June 1801), *"Briefe über Wien"* at 303-07, printing an account dated April 17, 1801.

[44] Beethoven to Franz Anton Hoffmeister in Leipzig, April 22 [1801], BGA No. 60: ". . . Thus I have composed a *ballet*, whereby however the *Ballet*master did not do his job all that well. . . " ("so habe ich ein *Ballet* gemacht, wobey aber der *Ballet*meister seine sache nicht ganz zum besten gemacht . . .").

[45] In Ritorni 1838, 89ff.; *see also* Applebaum 2002, at viii; Haas 1925, at 101-03. The 1813 version was in *six* acts, but used only a few of the numbers written by Beethoven (not including the finale), and drew on music by Haydn, Mozart, Weigl, and Gluck, as well as some by Viganò himself. See the account in Smart (2013), at 210-14; 226-30.

[46] *See* KH 102.

[47] For a general discussion of *opera seria, see* Grout 1965, ch. 14; for a broader view, *see* Dean 1969, ch. 1, at 5ff. The most famous definition of the genre, of course, comes from Samuel Johnson: in his "Life of John Hughes", *Lives of the English Poets* (vol. I, London, 1789), he wrote: "Italian opera [is] an exotick and irrational entertainment, which has been always combated, and always has prevailed . . .".

[48] Egon Voss (who is known chiefly as a musicologist) and Gunhild Schüller (Voss and Schüller 1997, at 501-02) categorically reject any allegorical reading of Viganò's scenario that attempts to relate it to Napoleon Bonaparte. They refer specifically to the influential monograph by Constantin Floros, *Beethovens Eroica und Prometheus-Musik* (Floros 1978). In that work, building on Fishman's initial analysis, Floros did the service of showing the

many musical connections between the *Prometheus* ballet and the *Eroica* (without, however, considering the piano variations that came between). He then essentially constructed the argument: Prometheus is to the ballet as Napoleon is to the Third Symphony; the Third Symphony is a further development of the ballet (with each movement corresponding to a scene in it); *ergo*, Napoleon must be at the root of the ballet as well—thereby transforming it into a species of "heroic" ballet (pp. 105-115). Floros supported his analysis by citing (among other contemporary works whose subject was Bonaparte) Vincenzo Monti's epic poem *Il Prometeo*, the first part of which was published in Bologna in 1797 and dedicated to Napoleon (*id.* at 46-48). To make his argument, however, Floros has to redefine the *genre* of ballet to which *Prometheus* belongs. This is where he runs afoul of the historians of dance, who are quite certain that the ballet was not what Floros contends, but just another in a long line of courtly *divertissements* (as Ritorni himself says [Appendix C, p. 96], in the sentence just before the last paragraph, and as the opening night reviewer also described the work [*see* pp. 19-20]). *See also* Goldschmidt 1975, 290-91.

[49] This was true as of 1801, at least, but Napoleon's ambitions set all politics in Europe greatly in flux. Seven years later, Franz II (now Emperor Franz I of Austria) would give his oldest daughter Sophia away to Napoleon in marriage. Maria Therese, whose hatred for Napoleon never ceased (Rice 2003, at 259-61), did not live to see that day; she had died after childbirth a year before.

[50] Voss and Schüller 1997. The tradition of such pieces goes back to the very beginnings of ballet, in the elaborate *masques* staged at Renaissance courts, and the courts of Henry VIII, Elizabeth I and James I. *See, e.g.,* Linton 2004. However, as Ritorni emphasizes (Appendix C, at p. 96; sentence before the last paragraph), the scenery, machinery and costumes of a *divertissement* like *Prometheus* were far smaller in scale than those used in, for example, the six-act version of the ballet produced by Viganò in Milan in 1813 (*see* n. 45).

[51] Beethoven's *Musik zu einem Ritterballett* (WoO 1), written in 1790-91 at Bonn, while already sufficient to distinguish him, is not on the level of *Die Geschöpfe des Prometheus*; the same is true of his two court cantatas written slightly earlier (WoO 87 and 88). However, Beethoven had gained valuable experience with operas, operettas and ballets in his years with the electoral theater in Bonn (*see* Hess 1962), so that in 1801 he could meet Viganò as an equal.

[52] Fleischhauer 1970; Witte 2003.

[53] The Prometheus myth is fully explored by Kerényi (1959). For an even broader survey of the multitude of treatments of the Prometheus myth in Europe, Trousson (2001) is indispensable. Walzel (1932) gives an overview of the myth in the German classical and romantic tradition, while Bertagnolli (2007) surveys its representations in the music of that period.

[54] The prologue was the first part of a two-part courtly ballet entertainment of the eighteenth century, as described by Voss and Schüller (1997).

[55] In Greek mythology, Amphion was such a master of the lyre that he helped his brother Zethus build the walls of Thebes—as he played his music, the stones responded by moving into place on their own. Arion was another master of the lyre, who is said to have composed the first dithyramb, or hymn of praise to Dionysus. He was noted for his escape, when sailors on the boat carrying him back from Italy tried to rob and kill him, on the back of a dolphin who was attracted by his singing.

[56] These elements formed the trilogy classically attributed to Aeschylus: *The Fire-Giver* (the bringing of the heavenly fire for mankind's benefit), *Prometheus Bound* (Prometheus' unjust punishment for helping mankind), and *Prometheus Unbound* (Prometheus surviving the punishment and being released). (There survive fragments of the first and third, and a text of the second, but both their authorship and their order are now disputed.) *See also* Kerényi 1959, at 77-128.

[57] BGA No. 60, quoted n. 44.

[58] Fishman, vol. III, at 47, sees an appeal that is wholly abstract, apart from the circumstances of Beethoven's life: "The composer saw the power of Prometheus—a proud and irreconcilable foe of tyranny—in his creative energy, in a life of action, in a high affirmation of human consciousness." Alan Tyson refuses to speculate: "What, if anything, did the figure of Prometheus mean to Beethoven: the fettered Titan hurling imprecations at Zeus? Or the ingenious craftsman who created men out of clay? . . . Unlike other works discussed here the subject matter may have meant nothing to him. Yet in June 1803, when his op. 35 variations were about to appear, he asked for the

theme's connection with *Prometheus* to be made explicit on the title-page (he was even prepared to pay the cost of re-engraving); and later in the year he returned to the theme once more for the finale of the *Eroica*" (Tyson 1969). Others, beginning with Goldschmidt (1975), at 30-33, Floros (1978), at 103-04, and continuing with Maruyama (1987), at 63-64, 78; Schneider (1988), at 69-75; Lockwood (2003), 150-51; and Schleuning and Geck (1989), 63ff., 93-96, as well as Schleuning (1987) and Hamilton-Paterson 2017, at 64-65, see Beethoven as drawn to the figure of Prometheus because the latter embodied the composer's classical ideals of heroism and of resisting tyranny; from this picture, an easy transference to the human figure of Napoleon is achieved. Mathews (1985), at 184-85, and Sipe (1998), at 19-20, both pick up one of the threads, but leave out the elements of enduring and then triumphing over an unjust punishment. *E.g.*, Sipe writes: "It may not be too much to maintain that, in the fall of 1802, Beethoven did regard himself as something of a Prometheus. Perhaps he saw his mission as that of the mythic Prometheus—the edification of humankind through art. . ." On another axis are Mosco Carner (1970) and Lewis Lockwood (2000; 2013), who each consider what the term "heroic" could mean in relation to the Third Symphony and subsequent works—without, however, referring to the ballet or to the figure of Prometheus. Both use Florestan as their paradigm; *e.g.*: "Beethoven may have seen in the wholly underserved suffering of Florestan his own undeserved suffering as an incurably deaf composer" (Carner 1970, at 361); "In that sense, I repeat, the hero as represented by Florestan is not the one who triumphs but rather the one who endures" (Lockwood 2000, at 43; *see also* Lockwood & Gosman 2013, vol. 1, at 30-32). Although they draw attention to the element of *enduring* undeserved suffering (as Beethoven also stressed in later correspondence [BGA No. 1292]), neither ties that element, or the other two elements of the heroic myth of Prometheus, into Beethoven's use of the term "*Eroica*". In essence, their inquiries start in the middle of the story, without regard for what preceded. In a similar vein, Gleich (1996), although making the identification between Beethoven's suffering and that of the Titan, views Beethoven's subsequent use of the theme in op. 35 and op. 55 as depicting exclusively the struggle of Prometheus himself as he seeks to get free of his chains, followed by music celebrating his triumphant restoration to freedom (pp. 9-10). He makes no connection between the music and the theme of human spiritual evolution as depicted in the ballet.

[59] *E.g.*, Riemann 1909-10; Mies 1953-54; Fishman, vol. III, 46-128; Floros 1978, at 82-104; Maruyama 1987, at 57-78.

162

[60] The one who comes closest to getting the balance about right is Kinderman (1995), at 86-90; even then, he focuses too much on Viganò's scenario, and thus misses the importance, in sustaining Beethoven through his suffering, of the elements of the classical myth which Viganò treated differently on stage. Witte (2003) lists all three elements of the myth in relation to Beethoven, but fails to follow the connections to the music, and uncritically summarizes previous scholarship. Much earlier, J.W.N. Sullivan had drawn the connection between the scheme of the *Eroica* Symphony and Beethoven's surmounting of his deafness. The funeral march of the second movement expressed the depth of Beethoven's despair at Heiligenstadt; the scherzo, his emergence with an "indomitable uprising of creative energy," and the finale, with its theme from *Prometheus,* indicated "the variety of achievement that is now open to his 'Promethean' energy" (Sullivan 1927, ch. 4, at 91). Sullivan makes no attempt, however, to analyze why Prometheus was important to Beethoven, or why Beethoven used the theme of the ballet finale in the last movement of the Symphony.

[61] Beethoven to Franz Wegeler, June 29, 1801 (BGA No. 65): " . . . I will, if it is otherwise possible, brave my fate, even though there will be moments of my life in which I will be the most miserable of God's creatures. . . " ("ich will wenn's anders möglich ist, meinen Schicksal trozen, obschon es Augenblicke meines Lebens geben wird, wo ich das unglucklichste Geschöpf gottes seyn werde. . . "); Beethoven to Carl Amenda, July 1, 1801 (BGA No. 67): " . . . but so must I withdraw from everything, my best years will fly away lost, without bringing to fruition all that to which my talent and my energy would have called me—[it is] melancholy *resignation* in which I must take my refuge. I have freely resolved to put myself beyond all of this, but how will it be possible?" (" . . . aber so von alles muß ich zurückbleiben, meine schönsten Jahre werden dahin fliegen, ohne alles das zu wirken, was mir mein Talent und meine Kraft geheißen hätten—traurige *resignation* zu der ich meine Zuflucht nehmen muß, ich habe mir Freylich vorgenommen mich über alles das hinaus zu sezen, aber wie wird es möglich seyn?")

[62] In the poem, Goethe expresses (in the voice of Prometheus) a profound disdain for the Greek gods who punished him:

163

Ich kenne nichts Ärmeres
Unter der Sonn als euch, Götter!
Ihr nähret kümmerlich
Von Opfersteuern
Und Gebetshauch
Eure Majestät
Und darbtet, wären
Nicht Kinder und Bettler
Hoffnungsvolle Toren.

Ich dich ehren? Wofür?
Hast du die Schmerzen gelindert
Je des Beladenen?
Hast du die Tränen gestillet
Je des Geängsteten?
Hat nicht mich zum Manne geschmiedet
Die allmächtige Zeit
Und das ewige Schicksal,
Meine Herrn und deine?
. . .
Hier sitz ich, forme Menschen
Nach meinem Bilde,
Ein Geschlecht, das mir gleich sei,
Zu leiden, zu weinen,
Zu genießen und zu freuen sich,
Und dein nicht zu achten,
Wie ich!

I know of nothing more wretched
Under the sun than you, Gods!
Beggarlike, you nourish—
From the sacrifices you impose,
And the wafting of prayers—
Your majesty,
And would starve, if
Children and beggars
Were not hopeless fools.

I honor you? For what?
Did you ever alleviate
The pains of the burdened?
Did you ever stop the tears
Of the anguished?
Did not omnipotent Time
Forge me into manhood,
And that eternal Fate,
My master and yours?
. . .
Here I sit, making humans
In my image,
A race made to resemble me:
To suffer, to weep,
To enjoy and to be happy,
And to scorn you,
As do I!

Although the poem's republican sentiment would have resonated with him, the command to be at eternal odds with the divine would have gone against Beethoven's firm sense of piety, which taught him to submit to his fate (*see* n. 61). As we will see,

Beethoven's *Prometheus* music expressed mankind's achievement in emulating the gods in art and music, not in scorning them.

[63] P. B. Shelley, *Prometheus Unbound,* act iv, lines 570-78 (1820).

[64] The letters previously cited in n. 61, along with a later letter to Wegeler (BGA No. 70): " . . . I will seize Fate by the throat, it certainly shall never bring me down completely" (" . . . ich will dem schicksaal in den rachen greifen, ganz niederbeugen soll es mich gewiß nicht"), and the Heiligenstadt Testament (BGA No. 106) provide abundant internal evidence of Beethoven's determination to meet his fate, endure it and conquer it.

[65] Tyson (1969) was the first to make this point in print (although not with regard to *Prometheus—see* n. 58); *see also* Tyson 1970, at 582-83, repr. Lang (ed.) 1971, at 79-80. The element of redemption through love is absent in the Prometheus myth, but it is represented in Viganò's ballet by the grief and concern expressed by the man and woman following Prometheus' supposed death, and by their jubilation when he rejoins them.

[66] Haas 1925; Sonnleithner (1861) informs us that the 1843 performance featured added music by Mozart and Haydn—a fact which does not surprise, since as Haas records, the 1843 revival was based on Viganò's scenario for the 1813 Milan production of the "big *Prometheus*" in six acts, and for which Viganò required much more music, including some he composed himself (*see* n. 45).

[67] *See* Plates 8 and 9, and n. 42.

[68] English translation taken from Senner, Wallace and Meredith (eds.) 1999, pp. 215-16. The original German text is given in Appendix D.

[69] August Kuhn, "Concert in Berlin", *Der Freymüthige* 23 (January 1826), 28. Translation from Senner, Wallace and Meredith (eds.) 1999, pp. 216-17.

[70] Fishman, vol. III, 47.

[71] Most of the German literature on the ballet credits Floros 1978 with the first full analysis of *Prometheus,* based on a review of all the sources. In fact, however, much of the credit should go to Nathan Fishman, who in pages 46-53 of his commentary (Fishman,

vol. III) first showed, using the sketches in Landsberg No. 7, the contrast Beethoven intended between the flowing music for Prometheus and for the first, halting steps of the humans. Fishman also analyzes the sketches for No. 9, where Prometheus is struck down by Melpomene, and for the finale, in which the humans finally evolve to the level of the gods. We owe to Floros the first comprehensive fitting together of all the known sources, in an attempt to reconcile some of Ritorni's ambiguities with those of the theater program. The analysis that follows, drawn on my 1966 thesis written twelve years before Floros' monograph, derives (except as noted) mainly from Fishman.

[72] Ritorni 1838, at 48 (Appendix C, p. 95 [beginning of second paragraph]).

[73] Opening night review (cited n. 68).

[74] For example, Ritorni (1838) says, at 49 (Appendix C, at 96): "Murder does not become an allegorical goddess, nor is it for Melpomene to be the agent of actual death, but only to act out catastrophes filled with blood. Why not rather depict, after the tragic end of man, the immortal life of the soul, the mercy of the deification of Prometheus, whom it suited Apollo, the god of action, to raise to immortal life?" ("Non conviene a divinità allegorica uccidere, nè a Melpomene dar morte vera, ma imitar vere catastrofi sanguinose. Perchè non rappresentar piuttosto, dopo il tragico fine dell'uomo, l'immortal vita dell'anima, mercè l'apoteosi di Prometeo, cui conveniva ad Apollo, nume dell'azione, innalzar a vita immortale?")

[75] Fishman, vol. III, at 51-52; Floros 1978, at 93-94; Maruyama 1987, at 58-59.

[76] Fishman, vol. III, 52.

[77] Floros 1978, at 69. The commentary here as to Nos. 10-15 is based on Floros and on my own subsequent research; Fishman's commentary on them is minimal.

[78] While the goal seems to have succeeded financially, it was not a success artistically. As quoted earlier (n. 68), the review described her dancing as "lackluster"; certainly she never captured the enthusiasm of the public as earlier had Madam Viganò. The other opening night review, in the *Journal des Luxus und der Moden* (n. 43), at p. 305), found her solo dancing "lacked character", and that her expression "at times bordered on the infantile".

⁷⁹ *See* Appendix C, at 96.

⁸⁰ "Weder Apoll noch einer der Musen, noch Bacchus, Pan oder Amphion und Orpheus, sondern die nun auf die Höhe ihrer Entwicklung gebrachten beiden Menschen sind die durch die Musik räpresentierten Helden." Riemann 1909-10, at 120. Fishman (after quoting Riemann) echoes him (Vol. III, 53): "[In the *Prometheus* melody, t]he awkwardness disappears, a gracefulness takes its place, the one-syllable motives change into an unbroken, broadly phrased melody which seems to express the general growth of man's spiritual beauty. . . . It is precisely in this high-principled context of the *Prometheus*-melody that the reason may be found for Beethoven's giving it a special place in his piano, ballet and symphonic work."

⁸¹ Stories abound of Beethoven's behavior toward nobles he thought were regarding him as an inferior; he smashed his bust of Prince Lichnowsky following one such incident (TDR II, 519-20; Thayer-Forbes, 403), and then purportedly wrote the Prince as follows (BGA, No. 258): "Prince, what you are, you are through chance and birth, what I am, I am through my own efforts; there has been and there will be thousands of Princes; but there is only one Beethoven." ("Fürst, was Sie sind, sind Sie durch Zufall und Geburt, was ich bin, bin ich durch mich; Fürsten hat es und wird es noch Tausende geben; Beethoven gibt's nur einen.") On Beethoven's "nobility pretense", *see* Solomon 1998, 117-20; also his earlier article (Solomon 1977).

⁸² The authorities so holding are reviewed and discussed in this chapter. Regarding the spelling "contredanse" in comparison the more English-looking alternative "contradance", I have chosen the former because (i) it is listed as the primary form, and (ii) it is closer to the German spelling (and equivalent to the French).

⁸³ Schindler 1860, vol. I, pp. 111-12; English tr. MacArdle (ed.) 1996, p. 118. The German of the passage quoted is: ". . . was . . . in der Schaar der Gegner besonderen Anstoß erregt hatte, war die Melodie im vierten Satze [der *Eroica*-Sinfonie]: [*Prometheus*-melody quoted] . . . die aus dem Finale des Balletts "Prometheus" noch in guter Errinerung gewesen. Die Tadler der Sinfonie frugen, wie dieselbe Melodie einmal zum Tanze, alsbald wieder zur Feier eines Helden benutzt warden könne? Viel früher aber war diese Melodie in einer Sammlung von Contretänzen da . . .".

[84] Schindler added these remarks on the origin of the Prometheus-melody between the publication of the error-ridden first edition of his Beethoven biography in 1841 and the much revised and expanded (but still error-prone) third edition in 1860. (A second edition of 1845 was a reprint of the first, with some added anecdotal and descriptive material not relevant here.) Why he thought it important to mention the criticisms of the *Eroica*'s "scores of enemies" in 1860, but not earlier, is known only to Schindler—who, after all, came on the scene nearly a decade after the Symphony's first performance, and a dozen years after the last performance of the ballet. As far as the present author has been able to determine, Schindler was, with this passage, the first to call attention to the link between the symphony and the contredanse.

[85] As is noted below (p. 46; text at n. 120), at least one contemporary reviewer treated the Basso del Tema as the principal theme of the Symphony's finale, and regarded the *Prometheus*-melody itself as counterpoint. A reviewer of the piano variations op. 35 does mention the source of the theme as the ballet, but that, of course, is no more than what Beethoven sought to have stated on their title page. ("Reviews", *Allgemeine musikalische Zeitung* 6 [February 22, 1804], 338-45.) The reviewer appears to have been familiar with the piano reduction of the ballet, published earlier.

[86] In his second edition of 1863 (Vol. I, at 198), Marx does mention the contredanse, and distances himself from Schindler by asserting that it came *after* the ballet (although he is not sure whether the dance predated the variations op. 35). It was doubtless this dispute in print to which Gustav Nottebohm had reference in his publication of the Kessler sketchbook a few years later (*see* quotation in n. 96).

[87] In his opinion for the Supreme Court in *New York Trust Co. v. Eisner* (1921) 256 U.S. 345, 349.

[88] In "Reviews and Literary Notices", *Atlantic Monthly* (March 1860). *See* Albrecht 1999.

[89] Thayer, vol. 2, 392-93.

[90] Lenz 1855/60, vol. III, 221-23.

[91] "Kann Hofrath Lenz Studien zu den Claviervariationen op. 35 mit denen zum Finale der *Eroica* verwechselt haben? Wenn nicht, dann bietet uns dieses Skizzenbuch die sehr

interessante Aufklärung: daß im Frühling [1801] Beethoven das Thema aus Prometheus für Orchestervariationen ausarbeitete; daß er im Herbst seine Absicht änderte und dasselbe zu Claviervariationen benutzte; daß er es im Winter in einem Contretanze verwendte (vielleicht um es bekannter zu machen?) und endlich im Jahre 1803 zu der ursprünglichen Idee der *Sinfonia Eroica* zurückkehrte und die Orchestervariationen als Finale ausarbeitete, den Trauermarsch hingegen, um die Stelle des langsamen Satzes einzunehmen." (Thayer, vol. 2, 392-93.)

Here Thayer has been misled by a number of earlier errors, as I explain in more detail in Appendix E (pp. 99-100).

[92] His notes on this point appeared posthumously, in the revised edition of volume II published in 1910 (TDR II, at 231-35) by Deiters' successor, Hugo Riemann. Note that Hugo Riemann has inserted Hermann Deiters' initials in the concluding sentence on page 235: "According to my [H. D.] belief, the sequence of the four settings of the E-Flat-Major theme is as follows: first contredanse, then *Prometheus*, then the variations [op. 35], then the *Eroica*." ("Nach meiner [H. D.] Überzeugung ist die Reihenfolge der vier Bearbeitungen des Es-Dur-Themas folgende: zuerst Kontretanz, dann *Prometheus*, dann Variationen, dann *Eroica*.") However, as we shall see (Appendix F, at 101), Riemann's careful attribution of the conclusion to Deiters did not mean that he disagreed with it.

[93] Based on a similar comparison, he concluded that the other contredanse (No. 11) which uses music from the ballet also had to precede the ballet version, because it was simpler in form as well (TDR II, 233-35). The sketches for the ballet, however, disprove this conclusion, as discussed later in this chapter. Moreover, Deiters has overlooked the fact that what he considers to be the "simpler" version of the contredanse (which he contrasts with measures 67-70 of the ballet score) is in fact used by Beethoven in the ballet finale, at measures 83-94, with different voicing.

[94] In the Kessler sketchbook, beginning with the octaves in half notes on page 83r (Brandenburg [ed.] 1978). *See* Figs. 22a and 22b. As the Kessler sketchbook shows, work on those variations did not commence before 1802—nearly a year after the premiere of the ballet, and several months after the first performance of the contredanse. In the course of that work, Beethoven saw that the bass line could be developed fugally, and the octave leap became an integral part of the fugue. (It also, as we shall see, figured prominently in the Wielhorsky sketches of the first draft for the first movement of the Third Symphony.) However, the variations op. 35 are not consistent; several of them do

not maintain the octave leap in the bass (*e.g.*, Var. III, IV, VI – IX, XI, XIII, and XV).

[95] Kojima 1980, 16-19.

[96] N1865 [Mies (ed.) 1924], at 42, n. 18: "The Variations Op. 35 were ready for print in December 1802. Another result ties in to this point. As everyone knows, Beethoven used the same theme which forms the basis for the Variations in yet three other compositions, namely in [the ballet] '*Prometheus*', in a collection of Contredanses and in the last movement of the *Sinfonia eroica*. The question of the chronological origin of these works has until now frequently been touched upon, but as it appears, not yet been definitively answered. The [Kessler] sketchbook [which Nottebohm is writing about] can assist with its resolution, because it relates to two of the named compositions, that is, toward its beginning with the Contredanses and later with the Variations, so that there can be no doubt over their chronological origin, or ordering. Now '*Prometheus*' (first performed in March 1801) belongs to an earlier time than that of the [Kessler] Sketchbook, while the *Sinfonia eroica* (completed in August 1804) belongs to a later time. Accordingly the chronological relationship can be simply established as follows: first '*Prometheus*', then the Contredanse, then the Variations Op. 35, and finally the *Sinfonia eroica*." ("Die Variationen Op. 35 waren druckfertig im Dezember 1802. Hieran knüpft sich noch ein Ergebniss. Beethoven hat bekanntlich dasselbe Thema, welches diesen Variationen zugrunde liegt, noch in drei andern Werken benutzt, nämlich in "Prometheus", in einer Sammlung von Contretänzen und im letzten Satz der *Sinfonia eroica*. Die Frage nach der chronologischen Enstehung dieser Werke ist bisher oft angeregt, aber, wie es scheint, noch nicht genau beantwortet worden. Das [Kesslersche] Skizzenbuch kann zu ihrer Lösung beitragen, da es mit zweien der genannten Werke in Berührung kommt, nämlich ziemlich zu Anfang mit den Contretänzen und später mit den Variationen, über deren chronologische Entstehung oder Aufeinanderfolge also kein Zweifel sein kann. Nun fällt ferner der "Prometheus" (aufgeführt zuerst im März 1801) in eine frühere Zeit, als das [Kesslersche] Skizzenbuch, und die *Sinfonia eroica* (vollendet im August 1804) in eine spätere Zeit. Demnach stellt sich das chronologische Verhältniss einfach heraus wie folgt: zuerst der "Prometheus", dann die Contretänze, dann die Variationen Op. 35, zuletzt die *Sinfonia eroica*.")

[97] These are described in Kerman (ed.) 1970, vol. 2, at 282; transcription on p. 72. *See also* N II, p. 229; Kojima 1980, at 17.

[98] The sketches are shown in Kerman 1970, vol. I, folios 50 and 154 (*see* Table II on p. xxvii). The copies of Nos. 8 and 12 in the autograph are described in KBK, p. 162, and in Kojima 1980, at 16.

[99] KBK, 162; Kojima 1980, 16. There we see that the final order as published was determined by Beethoven, who several times changed the order from that in the autograph by numbers written with the red pencil he used for corrections.

[100] The dedication "To Monsieur de Friederich, called 'Liederlich'" was evidently Beethoven's little joke: in German, "liederlich" means "dissolute", or "raffish".

[101] Recall that the Kessler sketchbook, which contains sketches for Nos. 10, 9 and 2, was used by Beethoven from October 1801 to May 1802. For this reason, Kojima (1980) concludes that the first part of the autograph score was not written down until the winter of 1801-02. Since it contains the only copy that we have of No. 7 in Beethoven's own hand, this section of the autograph is the strongest evidence there is that the contredanse was written after the ballet.

[102] Kojima (1980, at 16 and 18-19) offers a plausible explanation for this: the fourth section of the autograph was part of an earlier (but now missing) autograph prepared entirely by Karl for a set of six contredanses which he published under his own name in 1799 or 1800, no copies of which have come down to us. In doing so, he borrowed at least three (what we are calling Nos. 4, 8 and 12 of WoO 14) from his brother. When Ludwig came to assemble his own set of twelve contredanses for the 1801-02 season, he simply attached his brother's autograph rather than write them out again. (However, by the time he published the individual orchestra parts for publication in 1802, he had made significant corrections and improvements over what his brother had written.) *See also* Kojima 1977, at 311-14.

[103] KH 450-51.

[104] No. 11 was probably sent to the publisher at the last minute, once the duplication of No. 4 was discovered, in order to make a full set of twelve. Notice that in the printed order of the full score, No. 11 replaces the second occurrence of No. 4 in the autograph, just before the last dance, No. 12.

[105] Fishman, vol. III, at 53-54.

[106] *See* Mies 1925; Cooper 1990, 132-153.

[107] *See, e.g.,* Wade 1977; Reynolds 1982; Syer 2006.

[108] BGA No. 140. (". . . bey den großen *Variationen* ist noch Vergessen worden, daß das *Thema* davon aus einem von mir komponirten *allegorischen* Ballet nemlich: Prometheus oder *italienisch prometeo,* welches hätte auf das Titelblatt kommen sollen und wenn es möglich ist, bitte ich sie noch darum, d.h. im fall sie noch nicht herausgekommen, müsste das Titelblatt geändert werden, so geschehe es nur auf meine Kosten . . .")

[109] Fishman, vol. III, at 54.

[110] There is more to say about why subsequent Beethoven scholars have clung to the TDR chronology. The details are set out in Appendix F, at 101-103.

[111] Consider, for example, the explanation advanced by Thomas Sipe in his work on the *Eroica* Symphony (Sipe 1998). He delves briefly into the history of the contredanse as a folk form, and finds that it was uniquely popular among all social classes, so much so that when commoners were at the balls along with the nobility, and a contredanse was played, all the ranks would join in dancing it, and could freely mingle in executing its steps (*id.* at 12 and 19). As a dance in which all classes took part together, therefore, it was the appropriate vehicle for Beethoven to use in the *finale,* in which the human creatures joined with their creator and the other gods to celebrate their "graduation" from the academy of Parnassus. (*See also* Swafford 2014, at 267-68.)

       This argument, however, begs the question: why should Beethoven import into his ballet, out of twelve such contredanses, just Nos. 7 and 11, and no others? The evidence, as we have seen, demonstrates the reverse: both melodies were composed first for the ballet, and used afterwards for contredanses. In what I am calling the *Prometheus*-melody, through its use as a rondo theme, Beethoven had conceived the musical culmination of the humans' cultural evolution in the ballet. It expresses Prometheus' and his creatures' supreme joy at their having attained the ability to participate with the gods in celebrating their skill in the arts of music and dance. With the assumptions reversed in this fashion, notice how appropriate it becomes for Sipe's thesis, therefore, for Beethoven to adapt this sublime melody, along with another one used in the same finale, to a popular dance in which it was accepted that the bourgeois could consort with the nobility, and to include them in a set of twelve published for the very next ball season.

As an aside, it is not entirely clear that people freely mixed and changed partners in the contredanse. Sipe bases his description on a Ph.D. dissertation by Sarah Bennett Reichart of the City University of New York (Reichart 1984). A somewhat different perspective on the dance is given by Elizabeth Aldrich (Aldrich 1997). In contrast to Sipe and Reichart, Aldrich distinguishes the contredanse from the *anglaise*, or "englische", in which it was possible for people of different social levels to mix (much as early Americans would in dancing the Virginia reel, or a square-dance). Swafford (Swafford 2014, at 267) simply assumes that Beethoven adopted the *englische* form for the ballet because of its egalitarian character, but it is noteworthy that Beethoven himself never used that word to describe what he published as a "Contretanz". According to Aldrich, the contredanse in Vienna referred to a group dance for four to sixteen couples who executed complex steps, but who did not exchange partners (*id.* at 130-31). During the recent Mozart 250th anniversary festivities in Salzburg, the author watched a group of professional dancers perform a contredanse in 18th-century costumes. They executed the pattern of steps described by Aldrich, but one step did include—however briefly—a swap of partners. To add to the colorful mix of opinion on this point, John Rice (Rice 2003, at 125-27, 251) notes that the contredanse was one of the Empress Marie Therese's favorite dances, and that she even specified one in a ballet that she commissioned (whose description sounds like the dance described by Aldrich, and not by Reichart). Based on this fact, as well as on her previously undocumented role in getting Beethoven's *Fidelio* past the censors (*id.* at 252-58), Rice suspects that Marie Therese may have exercised some influence on Vigano's ballet scenario as well (*id.* at 248-51).

[112] Not every Beethoven scholar has taken up the bait offered by KH and TDR. Barry Cooper (Cooper 2000, at 111-12) is explicit that the contredanse could not have come first, given the evidence of the sketches; *see also* his straightforward treatment of the issue in Cooper 1999. Maynard Solomon (Solomon 1998, at 247) asserts simply that the ballet finale was "the earliest use" of the theme of the *Eroica* finale; Arnold Schmitz recites the correct order of composition (Schmitz 1927, at 102, probably relying on Nottebohm), as does both Romain Rolland (Rolland 1929, at 68), and Paul Bekker (Bekker 1912, at 223). The latest addition to this list is the composer and biographer Jan Swafford, who observes simply that by the time Beethoven began work on the piano variations op. 35, he had by then "also" used the theme of the ballet's finale in a set of contredanses (Swafford 2014, at 297). As the citations in Appendix F indicate, however, this has been the minority view to

date. In the middle is Constantin Floros, who takes note of the controversy but offers no opinion on its resolution (Floros 1978, at 72 n. 39; Eng. Tr. 2013, at 100 n. 38).

[113] On this point, *see generally* Burnham 1995, ch. 1; Sipe 1998, ch. 4.

[114] BGA, No. 108.

[115] Fishman, vol. III, at 65.

[116] *See* the Kessler sketchbook (Brandenburg [ed.] 1978), beginning with the octaves in half notes on page 83r; Reynolds 1982, at 50ff.

[117] Fishman, vol. III, 66; Maruyama 1987, at 79-80; Cooper 2000, at 133; *see also* Schleuning and Geck 1989, at 112-15, 151-61. In contrast, Smart (2013), at 220-26, sees "a more complicated interdependence of the gestural and the heroic-symphonic registers," in which Beethoven kept the treble of the Prometheus theme for its lyric, gestural character apart from the bassline, "made bizarre and cryptic when broken apart from its melody. The musical process – the separation of melody from its undedrgirding – embodies the way a musical utterance can be gradually brought into being, and thus conceptually seems to depict or allude to the transition from inert matter to living being, and, perhaps, the animation of the statues." This seems to focus more on the process than on its goal, which was to celebrate mankind's arrival at emulating the gods themselves in the arts of music and dance – with (for Beethoven) its personal connection to his surmounting the punishment of going deaf, by bringing forth music the likes of which no one at that time had ever heard before.

[118] It should be borne in mind, however, that Beethoven's first sketches of the bass theme separately are given as half notes, in 2/4 time—*see* Fig. 22a/b.

[119] Sonnleithner 1861; *see* discussion in Ch. 2, p. 10, text at n. 39.

[120] "Review", *Allgemeine musikalische Zeitung* 9 (February 18, 1807), 321-33; Eng. tr. in: Senner, Wallace and Meredith (eds.) 2001, No. 149, 20-32, at 26f.

[121] Reynolds 1982; *see* his Table 1, at p. 51.

[122] Fishman, vol. III, 83.

[123] In Mies 1953-54, at 97ff; Schenker 1930, 75; Fischer 1949; Lockwood 1991; Gleich 1996.

[124] The details are given in Appendix II to Reynolds 1982.

[125] Fishman also shows how Beethoven used ideas from his sketches for op. 35 in still other works, such as in the Piano Sonata Op. 31, No. 3 (Fishman, vol. III, 147-48).

[126] Fishman, vol. III, 77.

[127] Fishman, vol. III, 76.

[128] Fishman, vol. III, 78.

[129] Douglas Johnson *et al.* report that there are eight separate leaves of sketches for *Christus am Oelberge,* op. 85 which at one time were part of the Wielhorsky sketchbook, plus a ninth leaf which has not been located (JTW 131-32). Thus as originally bound, the sketchbook would have had 192 pages.

[130] Reynolds 1982, at 63-72; Brandenburg (ed.) 1978, vol. I, at 33-34.

[131] Wegeler/Ries, 82-83.

[132] BGA No. 103.

[133] BGA No. 104.

[134] BGA No. 107. The publication of the Wielhorsky sketches has allowed scholars to resolve the issue of the number of variations which Karl claims for each set in this letter. Fishman, vol. III, 72-73; Cooper 2000, at 118.

[135] *See* BGA Nos. 108, 123, 127, 128, and 133.

[136] Wegeler/Ries, 98-99: "Beethoven litt nämlich schon im Jahr 1802 verschiedenemal am Gehör, allein das Übel verlor sich wieder. Die beginnende Harthörigkeit war für ihn eine

so empfindliche Sache, daß man sehr behutsam sein mußte, ihn durch lauteres Sprechen diesen Mangel nicht fühlen zu lassen. Hatte er etwas nicht verstanden, so schob er es gewöhnlich auf eine Zerstreutheit, die ihm allerdings in höherem Grade eigen war. Er lebte viel auf dem Lande, wohin ich denn öfter kam, um meine Lection zu erhalten. Zuweilen sagte er dann, Morgens um acht Uhr nach dem Frühstück: "Wir wollen erst ein wenig spazieren gehen." Wir gingen, kamen aber mehrmals erst um 3 – 4 Uhr zurück, nachdem wir auf irgendeinem Dorfe etwas gegessen hatten. Auf einer dieser Wanderungen gab Beethoven mir den ersten auffallenden Beweis der Abnahme seines Gehörs, von der mir schon Stephan von Breuning gesprochen hatte. Ich machte ihn nämlich auf einen Hirten aufmerksam, der auf einer Flöte, aus Fliederholz geschnitten, im Walde recht artig blies. Beethoven konnte eine halbe Stunde hindurch gar nichts hören, und wurde, obschon ich ihm wiederholt versicherte, auch ich höre nichts mehr, (was indeß nicht der Fall war,) außerordentlich still und finster. . . ."

[137] Fishman, vol. III, 108-28. *See* my partial translation of these pages in Appendix G, pp. 106-132.

[138] Quoted pp. 32-33 (text at n. 91).

[139] Appendix E, 99-100.

[140] Lenz 1855/60, vol. III, at 222-23.

[141] Nohl 1874, at 95-101.

[142] *Id.* at 98: "welches wieder von unserm Bleistiftmann mit '*Eroica*' bezeichnet ist!"

[143] *Id.* at 99: ". . . sondern auf Symphonie oder Quartett zu schließen ist. Die Skizzen des Menuetto füllen auch noch S. 45 aus."

[144] Fishman, vol. III, 110-128; Floros 1978, 78f.; Lockwood 1981, at 460-61, repr. Lockwood 1992, at 136. It is interesting to note that in 1810, Bettina von Brentano described Beethoven's method as follows (Letter dated July 9, 1810 to Anton Bihler, in Würz and Schimkat [eds.] 1961, 188-89): "[Beethoven] does not proceed like Kapellmeister Winter, who writes down whatever first occurs to him: he first makes a grand plan and then arranges his music into a particular form, toward which he later works." ("Er macht's

nicht wie der Kapellmeister Winter, der hinschreibt, was ihm zuerst einfiel; er macht erst großen Plan und richtet seine Musik in eine gewisse Form, nach welcher er nachher arbeitet.")

[145] Nottebohm (N1880 [Mies (ed.) 1924], p. 4) noted that there were five missing leaves near the very beginning of Landsberg No. 6 when he examined it; perhaps these contained earlier drafts of the first movement. (Lockwood & Gosman 2013 [vol. 1, at 9-11] draw on a fresh examination of the sketchbook to surmise that it was Beethoven himself who removed the leaves, perhaps to satisfy an urgent need for music paper.) Nevertheless, Fishman (vol. III, at 110-28) is able to connect the Wielhorsky sketches with those in Landsberg No. 6 quite well. His detailed analysis of the sketches on pp. 44-45 of Wielhorsky shows how the so-called "new" E-minor theme of the first movement's development section (in Landsberg No. 6) originated from the secondary theme of the Wielhorsky sketches, how the famous dominant-tonic clash just before the recapitulation was already contemplated in the Wielhorsky sketches, and he shows much that connects the Wielhorsky sketches for the second and third movements with their counterparts in Landsberg No. 6 as well. (On these points, compare the analysis of Lewis Lockwood, which corroborates the connections made by Fishman [Lockwood & Gosman 2013, vol. 1, at 32-35].) His report to the International Musicological Congress in Berlin 1970 (Fischman 1970) gives a brief summary of his findings in German, but his Russian commentary on the sketches has yet to be published in English translation. (A partial translation is given in Appendix G.)

[146] BGA Nos. 65 and 67.

[147] From BGA No. 65: ". . . ich habe schon oft den schöpfer und mein daseyn verflucht, Plutarch hat mich zu der Resignation geführt, ich will wenn's anders möglich ist, meinem schicksaal trozen, obschon es Augenblicke meines Lebens geben wird, wo ich das unglücklichste Geschöpf gottes seyn werde." Notice the reference to Geschöpf— Beethoven is regarding his relation to his creator as akin to that of the animated clay figures to Prometheus.

[148] BGA No. 70.

[149] Solomon 1998, at 196-97.

[150] Quoted at p. 32.

[151] BGA No. 165.

[152] TDR II, 261ff.; Thayer-Forbes, 309ff.

[153] Cooper 1995; *see also* Tyson 1970, at 551, 582-84, repr. Lang 1971, at 49, 79-82. Cooper makes the case for a transferal of Beethoven's anguish at Heiligenstadt to the suffering of Jesus depicted in the oratorio, on which Beethoven presumably worked from November 1802 to March 1803. While I certainly do not disagree that such a transferal occurred, it is noteworthy that it happened *after* Beethoven's resort to the *Prometheus*-music to get him through his period of despair at Heiligenstadt, and in the interim before he resumed work on the *Eroica*. (The story is then continued by Beethoven's taking up the subject of Florestan in *Fidelio*—*see* the articles by Lewis Lockwood and Mosco Carner cited in n. 58).

[154] Lockwood 1981, at 469, repr. Lockwood 1992, at 143.

[155] N1880 [Mies (ed.) 1924], 6-18. Katherine Syer (Syer 2006, at 172-78) thinks that the sketches for the Marches for Piano (op. 45) which are in the *Eroica* Sketchbook at pp. 44-48, and which are surrounded by sketches for the second movement of the *Eroica*, were written while Beethoven was at Heiligenstadt in 1802; if so, this could mean that Beethoven continued work on the *Eroica* in late 1802, but in Landsberg No. 6 rather than in Wielhorsky. For an extensive discussion, based on the sketches of 1802 and 1803, of how the *Eroica* reached its final form, *see* Swafford (2014), ch. 17 (pp. 331ff.).

[156] Harry Goldschmidt (Goldschmidt 1975), at 32, sees in the sequence *Marcia funebre* – Scherzo – horn trio a recapitulation of Nos. 9, 10 and 11/12 in the ballet: tragic muse – comic muse – Pan and his followers.

[157] TDR II, 403; Thayer-Forbes, 337. The guest was the artist Josef Willibrord Mähler, whose later portrait of the young Beethoven (ca. 1804) is in the Pasqualati House of the Vienna Museum.

[158] *See* text at p. 45, n. 117.

[159] Letter from Ries to Simrock, October 22, 1803 (BGA No. 165).

[160] Letter from Ries to Simrock, August 6, 1803 (BGA No. 152).

[161] Letter from Ries to Simrock, December 11, 1803 (BGA No. 173).

[162] Volek and Macek 1986; Albrecht (ed.) 1996, vol. 1, No. 81. A correspondent of Dohms and Rodenbergs *Salon* II, Heft 9 wrote (TDR II, 426 n. 1): ". . . a contemporary and—even more—a member [of Lobkowitz's court orchestra] claimed that Lobkowitz had formed his orchestra precisely with the purpose that Beethoven could try out his works before their publication!" (". . . ja ein Zeitgenosse und sogar Mitglied [der Kapelle von Lobkowitz] behauptet, Lobkowitz habe die Kapelle ganz eigens zu dem Zwecke gebildet, um die Werke Beethovens vor ihrer Veröffentlichung zuerst zu versuchen!") Apart from this, Peter Schleuning suggests that Prince Lobkowitz had heard of Beethoven's plans to dedicate the Symphony to Napoleon and to move to Paris, and intervened to keep both Beethoven and his Symphony in Vienna (Schleuning 1996, at 395-96).

[163] Wegeler/Ries, 78-79 (Eng. tr., 68).

[164] BGA No. 181.

[165] BGA No. 188.

[166] The score is preserved today, along with the oldest known set of orchestral parts, in the Library of the Gesellschaft der Musikfreunde in Vienna. *See* Tusa 1985.

[167] The piano sonata in F Major, op. 54, was not published until April 1806 (KH 127).

[168] *E.g.*, the reviewer in *Der Freymüthige* 3 (April 17, 1805) noted that the audience for the premiere divided into three camps: "The first group, Beethoven's very special friends, maintains that exactly this Symphony is a masterpiece, which is in the true style of higher music, and if it does not please for the present, that is because the public is not sufficiently educated in art to grasp all its finer points; but after a couple of thousand years it would not fail to have its effect. The second group denies the work any artistic merit whatsoever, and believes there to be visible in it an unrestrained striving for notice and strangeness, which has nowhere led to beauty, or to true grandeur or power. By means of unusual modulations and forceful transitions, by juxtaposing the most

heterogeneous things, as when—for example—a Pastorale is performed in the heaviest style, with a lot of scratchings in the bass, with three horns and so forth, a certain if not exactly desirable originality can, to be sure, be achieved without much difficulty. Genius, however, authenticates itself not by the bringing forth of that which is merely unusual and fantastic, but rather that which is beautiful and sublime: Beethoven himself proved the truth of this statement in his earlier works. The third—very small—group is in the middle. It allows that the Symphony has many beautiful points, but recognizes that its coherence often appears to be rent asunder, that the unending duration of this longest and perhaps most difficult of symphonies will exhaust even connoisseurs, and prove unbearable to mere amateurs. It wishes that Mr. v. B. would use his admittedly great talents to present us with works that were like his first two symphonies in C and D, his charming Septet in E-Flat, his witty Quintet in D [C?], and others among his earlier compositions, which will put Beethoven forever in the first rank of instrumental composers. This group fears, however, that if Beethoven strides further down this path, both he and the public will thereby fare badly. Music could quickly reach the point that everyone who is not well versed in the rules and difficulties of art will find no kind of enjoyment in it whatsoever, but instead, pressed to the floor by a crowd of unconnected and superfluous ideas, and by a perpetual tumult of all the instruments, will leave the concert hall with only unpleasant feelings of fatigue. The public and Mr. v. Beethoven, who conducted the work himself, were not satisfied with each other. For the public the symphony was too difficult and too long, and Beethoven himself was too impolite, because he bestowed no nod of his head even on those who were applauding. For his part, Beethoven found the applause insufficient."

("Die einen, Beethoven's ganz besondere Freunde, behaupten, gerade diese Sinfonie sei ein Meisterstück, das sei eben der wahre Styl für die höhere Musik, und wenn sie jetzt nicht gefällt, so komme das nur daher, weil das Publicum nicht kunstgebildet genug sei alle diese hohen Schönheiten zu fassen; nach ein paar tausend Jahren aber würde sie ihre Wirkung nicht verfehlen. – Der andere Theil spricht dieser Arbeit schlechterdings allen Kunstwerth ab und meint, darin sei ein ganz ungebändigtes Streben nach Auszeichnung und Sonderbarkeit sichtbar, das aber nirgends Schönheit oder wahre Erhabenheit und Kraft bewirkt hätte. Durch seltsame Modulationen und gewaltsame Uebergänge, durch das Zusammenstellen der heterogensten Dinge, wenn z. B. ein Pastorale im größten Style durchgeführt wurde, durch eine Menge Risse in den Bässen, durch drei Hörner u. a. d. könne zwar eine gewisse eben nicht wünschenswerthe Originalität ohne viele Mühe gewonnen werden; aber nicht die Hervorbringung des blos Ungewöhnlichen und Phantastischen, sondern des Schönen und Erhabenen sei es, wodurch sich das Genie beurkunde: Beethoven hatte selbst durch seine früheren Werke die Wahrheit dieses Satzes erwiesen. – Die dritte sehr kleine Partie steht in der Mitte; sie gesteht der Sinfonie manche Schönheiten zu, bekennt aber, daß der Zusammenhang oft ganz zerrissen scheint, und daß die unendliche Dauer dieser längsten, vielleicht auch schwierigsten aller Symphonieen selbst Kenner ermüde, dem bloßen Liebhaber aber unerträglich werde. Sie wünscht, daß H. v. B. seine anerkannten großen Talente verwenden möge, uns Werke zu schenken, die seinen beiden ersten Symphonieen aus C und D gleichen, seinem anmuthigen Septett aus Es, dem geistreichen Quintett aus D dur [C-dur?] und anderen seiner früheren Compositionen, die B. immer in die Reihe der ersten Instrumentalcomponisten stellen werden. Sie fürchtet aber, wenn Beethoven auf diesem Wege fort wandelt, so werde er und das Publicum übel dabei fahren. Die Musik könne so bald dahin kommen, daß jeder, der nicht genau mit den Regeln und Schwierigkeiten der Kunst vertraut ist, schlechterdings gar kein Genuß bei ihr finde, sondern durch eine Menge unzusammenhängender und überhäufter Ideen und einen fortwährenden Tumult aller Instrumente zu Boden gedrückt, nur mit einem unangenehmen Gefühle der Ermattung den Conzertsaal verlasse. Das Publicum und H. v. Beethoven, der selbst dirigirte, waren an diesem Abende nicht mit einander zufrieden. Dem Publicum war die Symphonie zu schwer, zu lang, und B. selbst zu unhöflich, weil er auch den beifallklatschenden Theil keines Kopfnickens würdigte. Beethoven im Gegentheile fand den Beifall nicht auszeichnend genug.")

The incident of Beethoven's failure to acknowledge his public at this concert was picked up and gently satirized by Joseph Richter in his *Eipeldauerbriefe* (Richter 1785-1813, reprinted Paunel and Gugitz, ed. 1917-1918, vol. II, at 203), in which he reported: "On Palm Sunday a wonderful concert took place at the Theater an der Wien, and afterward they gave special applause to a gentleman who wrote some of the music, but because he acknowledged their huge applause only with a slight nod of his head, some of them have discussed the matter with each other, and put the thing down to an artist's hauteur; but the gentlemen will scarcely have known that the good Herr composer had just on that day a bit of rheumatism in his neck, and so couldn't bow any deeper." ("An Palmsonntag ist aufn Theater an der Wien ein wunderschöne Akademi gebn worden, und da habn s' bsonders einen Herrn zuklascht, der einen Theil der Musik gmacht hat, weil er aber für den großen Beyfall nur mit ein klein Kopfducker dankt hat, so habn sich einige drüber aufgehalten, und habn das Ding für ein Künstlerstolz ausglegt; aber die Herrn werden's halt nicht gwußt habn, das der brave Herr Kompositor grad denselben Tag ein Rematismi in Gnack ghabt hat, und da hat er sich ja nicht tiefer bucken können.")

[169] BGA No. 226.

[170] BGA, No. 223.

[171] Shelley, *Prometheus Unbound,* act iv, quoted at 19.

[172] Notice that this scheme could work only in connection with his planned move to Paris. Once Beethoven decided to stay in Vienna, he could no more publicly dedicate a major work to an enemy of the state than he could have composed a set of variations on *La Marseillaise.* The proof is in what actually happened: the dedication in 1806 went instead to Prince Lobkowitz, an acknowledged patriot who raised at his own expense troops to fight Napoleon's armies (*see* Plate 1, p. ix).

[173] Thus according to an anecdote related by the poet Christoph Kuffner (TDR IV, 29; Thayer-Forbes, 674).

Made in United States
North Haven, CT
23 May 2022

19450141R00107